WOMAN ENTREPRENEUR
Extraordinaire

Top Experts Share Their Secrets
for More Business Success

THRIVE
PUBLISHING™

THRIVE Publishing
A Division of PowerDynamics Publishing, Inc.
San Francisco, California
www.thrivebooks.com

ISBN: 978-0-9836395-8-9

Library of Congress Control Number: 2011942334

Printed in the United States of America on acid-free paper.

URL Disclaimer
All Internet addresses provided in this book were valid at press time.
However, due to the dynamic nature of the Internet, some addresses
may have changed or sites may have changed or ceased to exist since
publication. While the co-authors and publisher regret any
inconvenience this may cause readers, no responsibility for any
such changes can be accepted by either the co-authors or the publisher.

We dedicate this book to you

the entrepreneur, business owner, sales professional or consultant, whether you are experienced or are just starting out on your path to entrepreneurship. You recognize the power of knowing what to do, as well as how and when to do it in order to be wildly successful. We salute you for wanting more knowledge designed to advance your business—and we celebrate your commitment to being the best you can be. We are here to give you all we have to make your entrepreneurial venture extraordinary.

The Co-Authors of *Woman Entrepreneur Extraordinaire*

Table of Contents

Acknowledgements

Gratitude is an important part of business success. Before we share our wisdom and experience with you, we have a few people to thank for turning our vision for this book into a reality.

This book is the brilliant concept of Caterina Rando, the founder of Thrive Publishing™ and a respected business speaker and strategist. Without Caterina's "take action" spirit, her positive attitude and her commitment to excellence, you would not be reading this book, of which we are all so proud.

Additionally, a truly dedicated team has worked diligently to put together the best possible book for you and supported all of our efforts. We are grateful for everyone's stellar contribution.

To Patricia Haddock, whose experience in copywriting and copy-editing proved invaluable, and whose magic pen and expertise ensured that this book would be the best it could be.

To Tricia Principe, Barbara McDonald, and Tammy Tribble, our designers extraordinaire, who brought their creative talents to the cover and book layout, thank you all for your enthusiasm, problem solving and attention to detail throughout this project.

To our exceptional proofreaders, Tony Lloyd and Rua Necaise, thank you for ensuring we dotted all the i's, crossed all the t's and placed every comma where it belongs.

We also acknowledge each other for delivering outstanding information, guidance and advice to you. Through our work in this book and with our clients, we are truly committed to enhancing the success of women entrepreneurs throughout the world. We are grateful that we get to do work that we love and contribute to so many in the process. We do not take our good fortune lightly. We are clear in our mission—to make a genuine contribution to you, the reader. Thank you for granting us this extraordinary opportunity.

The Co-Authors of *Woman Entrepreneur Extraordinaire*

Introduction

Congratulations! You have opened an incredible resource, packed with great ideas that will enhance your entrepreneurial experience in ways you cannot yet imagine. You are about to discover how to strengthen and develop your business skills to ensure that your business is profitable, sustainable and thriving.

Your success comes as the result of more than talent, commitment and hard work. Your success will also be determined by how well you manage all aspects of your business. When you are an entrepreneur, you are responsible for everything—marketing, product development, customer service, sales and networking. Every success and setback you experience will come from the decisions you make. Your success as an entrepreneur depends on how productively and effectively you run your business and how well you communicate and cultivate customer relationships and strategic alliances.

We know you want to be the absolute best entrepreneur you can be. With this book, you will quickly learn how successful women entrepreneurs get the very best results. As top experts in each of our respective specialties, we have joined to give you the most powerful information and strategies available.

Each of us has seen how even small changes can transform and uplift a business. Here is just a sample of the benefits you will find inside to transform yours:

- Communicate your personal brand and make it part of everything you do.

- Avoid legal mistakes that can cost you not just money, but your business as well.

- Plan financially for both professional and personal success.

- Dispel negative beliefs that can undermine your success.

- Create information products and cash flow.

- And much more.

All the entrepreneurs you will meet in this book want you to succeed. We have outlined for you our top strategies and included the most expert advice we have to advance your success.

To get the most out of *Woman Entrepreneur Extraordinaire,* we recommend you read it once, cover to cover, then go back and follow the advice that applies to you in the chapters most relevant to your current situation. Every improvement you make will increase your confidence and effectiveness and positively affect how others respond to your business.

Just learning what to do will not create transformation. Take action and apply the strategies, tips and tactics we share in these pages, and you will reap many rewards. With our knowledge and your action, we are confident that, like our thousands of satisfied clients, you too will benefit from *Woman Entrepreneur Extraordinaire.*

To your unlimited success!

The Co-Authors of *Woman Entrepreneur Extraordinaire*

Exemplifying Authenticity and Excellence as an Entrepreneur

Let Your Life Shine

By Lisa Centamore Sinkiewicz

*E*xemplifying authenticity and excellence as an entrepreneur is the result of being your true self. The journey of self-discovery is a lifelong process that often begins during our childhood. I remember as a young girl, my dad would tell me stories at night before bed, and I would be off in a land of imagination. Where would I travel? Who would I become? What great things would I accomplish? My dad breathed life into all of these visions for me, and I learned the power of a forward-focused imagination! Although the journey of finding one's true self is not as simple as closing our eyes and just imagining it, these seeds planted the desire to learn more about myself. Nothing was impossible—thus began the journey of discovering the core of my being.

When you define your values and set your goals and priorities according to them, your business will shine with excellence because it is an extension of your true self. Your business will flourish and thrive with you as the core of its workings. Those you meet through your business will want to work with you because of who you are and what you represent. You will no longer live the dichotomy of who you are "at home" versus who you are "at work,"—this will bring you more fulfillment and satisfaction. Embracing the strengths you have within allows you to be transparent and shows your best in every moment of each day. Embrace this chapter and allow it to support you in defining your true self as an entrepreneur. Allow yourself to build excellence and shine in your business by bringing out the best of who you are in alignment with your values.

> *"Set your expectations high, use the skills you've acquired and unlock the door to your dreams."*
> —Gwen Ifill, American journalist, television newscaster and author

Know Your Values

Through moments of profound reflection, internal truths that come from your coaching experiences and learning through reading and explorations, your journey will take place. It will expose the answer to the intuitive questions revolving around who you want to become, what legacy you would like to inspire and what you want to be known for. By searching deep within your heart, you will uncover your values and the strength to live according to them. Awareness of your values empowers you to live authentically as your best self and, through that, lead as an example of excellence within your business and with those you encounter.

Essentially, defining your values gives clarity on what is important to you and allows you to spend your time in the most productive ways to support your standards. In addition, once you know your values, you can prioritize your goals, so the ones that support your higher values are given precedence. Identifying and prioritizing both your values and your goals brings you one step closer to living the life you have imagined.

Ask yourself these questions:

- When do you feel most fulfilled and what value does this support in your life?

- How do you describe your "best" life?

- What are your values? What things do you hold in the core of your being that are most important to your way of living?

- How do you measure your priorities and the quality of your life?

Often, the times we are most fulfilled and at our happiest are the times when we are aligned with our values. Have you ever sat and considered what your values might be? Quiet yourself, read the following questions, then close your eyes and consider your answers.

- When do you feel most at peace and which values are being honored at those times?

- How do you want people to describe you to others?

- If you were to describe the person you want to become, what words come to mind?

Close your eyes and when you are ready, open them. Look at the partial list of values below and circle ten that speak to you most clearly. You may also brainstorm values not on this list that you want to exhibit and uphold in your life and your business.

Abundance	Acceptance	Achievement	Affection
Balance	Bravery	Charity	Consistency
Creativity	Family	Freedom	Generosity
Gratitude	Growth	Honesty	Integrity
Joy	Love	Optimism	Passion
Peace	Perseverance	Poise	Presence
Respect	Self-Control	Teamwork	Trust
Vision	Wisdom		

Now, list the values you selected in order of importance to you. Review your list and ask yourself, "If I could only be known for one, which would I choose?" This is an important step because prioritizing your values gives you the freedom to live with goals that support what is most important. In this way, your business becomes a reflection of your values as well.

With a clear view of your values, you can now transform your values into a way of life and excellence in your business. Examine your business and the elements of it that support your values. Then generate a list of ways that you can more fully live in alignment with those values and begin to implement these ideas daily into your business practices. Refer back to your values list to be sure your goals support your values, so you are experiencing realness and peace in all you do.

Following these steps is not a quick process and requires much introspection. Take your time as you move through this inquiry and enjoy the journey. Following this process will set the foundation for all future movement as you intentionally build excellence as an entrepreneur. It is amazing how knowing your values gives you permission to not worry about minor details and to live each moment in the present. This is another step forward in living authentically.

> *"The great and glorious masterpiece of humanity*
> *is to know how to live with purpose."*
> —Michel de Montaigne, French writer and essayist

Define Your Mission and Purpose

Your mission and purpose state the reason for your work. Why do you want to set out on this journey as an entrepreneur? How can you make a difference and what can you give back to the world? Your purpose helps you to see how your contribution makes a difference in the lives of others.

Above all, your mission and purpose will inspire you! Your purpose will unveil all that you need to create the life and business of your dreams. What is the true meaning and purpose you have within you? For me, my purpose was to help inspire others to be their authentic selves and to be a role model of excellence for my children. In doing so, I know that leading by example is causing a ripple effect, and I am giving back to the world one person at a time.

Create an Inspiring Vision

The visions you have today become tomorrow's realities, so allow yourself to dream big. Every invention and every advancement of the past has been the result of one person's vision. Your vision acts as a springboard for future successes and makes your legacy unique. Holding high expectations for yourself enables you to tap into your creative side to see what you could really do if there were no limits on your visions. The rewards of having a vision are infinite. These questions can help you clarify your vision:

• What are your dreams and the wishes of your life?

• If you close your eyes and look forward five to ten years, what does your life look like?

• What does it feel like?

• What milestones have you reached?

Dream in details with colors, sights, smells and sounds to imagine every detail of this vision. Your visions are your life's ambition!

Sit quietly and write down each of your visions as if it already has happened. Keep a journal, so you can add details. Map out the steps you need to turn your visions into reality. Make a vision board that represents where you want to go and what you want to become. Use words and pictures to create your board and hang it in your office to serve as a constant reminder of your visions. Surround yourself with inspiring quotes, words and readings that support your goals. Live as if these visions have already happened and work backwards to create an action plan to achieve them. Writing them down creates a self-fulfilling prophecy.

> *"What the mind can believe, you can achieve."*
> —Lorraine Moller, New Zealand athlete

Work with Intention

A vision without work is only a dream. You must build on your dreams with belief in each of your visions and take the final and most important step to work toward bringing them to life. In order to make them realities, you need to set goals and create an action plan.

Work in alignment with your values to prevent burnout and live more fully. This clarity will allow you to view obstacles as opportunities and give you the ability to rise above adversity. When you know your intentions, you will have fewer excuses and will seek more solutions. As your values become the source of your intentions, time management becomes easier because you plan according to your priorities. Your goals support your values—by keeping your values central, you experience balance and fulfillment in your life.

Goal setting is the roadmap that determines your course of success. Be sure your goals are specific and measurable with a deadline. Each time you create and achieve a goal, you are taking one step toward reaching your vision. When your goals seem too large, break them down into smaller tasks and move into action. You will be motivated to keep progressing.

Accept that while working to achieve your visions, you will have setbacks and challenges. They do not need to stop you. Use them to gain clarity on your mission and purpose and reignite the passion for your visions. Although you may not know right now every step needed to achieve your visions, trust that each step you take will reveal the next step along the journey and that each step was necessary for you to reach your potential.

> *"The future belongs to those who*
> *believe in the beauty of their dreams."*
> —Eleanor Roosevelt, former first lady of the United States,
> diplomat and human rights activist

Believe It!

Now that you have laid the foundation with a purpose, a vision, goals and an action plan, *you must believe!* Know that you deserve to succeed and can manifest your visions.

Mike Dooley is an international speaker, philosophical author and the founder of TUT'S Adventurers Club online. Mike publishes *Notes from the Universe* daily. These messages focus on helping make dreams a reality and are designed to remind you of life's magic, your power and that dreams really do come true.

When you are in doubt, sit and reflect on the values that help you define who you are and what you want to give back to your world. Remind yourself of your reason for doing what you do and find the passion within yourself to live as an authentic being.

Believe that when your reasons and passion are strong enough, nothing will get in the way of you achieving your goals and that you have everything it takes to succeed on your journey!

Keep an Attitude of Gratitude

An attitude of gratitude is an essential element of success. It keeps you focused on the positive and gives you the strength to move beyond negativity, setbacks and challenges along your way.

Keep a gratitude journal. Start now by listing everything you are grateful for and then, at the end of each day, write down five blessings from that day or five reasons you are proud of yourself.

Control your thoughts with positive affirmations and surround yourself with quotes and passages that will inspire you to be thankful and abundant. The *Law of Attraction* is a metaphysical belief that "like attracts like," that positive and negative thinking bring about positive and negative results, respectively. When you focus on what you have and are grateful for, abundance prevails. A gratitude journal will help remind you to be thankful for your blessings and to view all in life as a blessing.

Stay Motivated

You are an average of the five people with whom you spend the most time, so be sure you are spending time with like-minded people who live by values similar to your own and who are moving in the direction of their goals.

You can use coaching, accountability partners and mentors within your field. Both individual and group coaching give you the opportunity to surface answers from within to grow your business.

A goal buddy or an accountability buddy is a person to share goals with and check in with consistently to evaluate the progress you have made towards your goals. In addition to providing accountability, a mentor can teach you and guide you along the journey in light of her experiences and the challenges she encountered throughout her own journey.

Lastly, continue to educate yourself in your field. Conferences and trainings arc vital to your success. You can never know too much!

> *"The more you praise and celebrate your life,*
> *the more there is in life to celebrate."*
> —Oprah Winfrey, American television host and philanthropist

Celebrate Your Successes

After reaching a goal, it is easy to just move on to the next goal—that is what high achieving women often do. However, it is vital to celebrate the joys of your success along the way. What makes you happy? What do you enjoy doing with your free time? By indulging in the pleasures that inspire you, you bring out the best of who you are in each moment, and you reinvigorate your spirit for the next climb. You can celebrate your successes with a shout out or a little dance in your office after you hang up the phone from a new sale. You can crack open a bottle of champagne, take your team to dinner or put a photo on the wall to commemorate your success. Pick what works for you. How are you going to celebrate your accomplishments?

Now that you have an idea of what authenticity and excellence is, it is your turn to define what that means for you! It is your turn to dream it, believe it and work it.

Sit and reflect over the next few days about your purpose and your work's mission. Ponder your list of values and manifest them in everything you choose to do as an entrepreneur. Consider what *your* life of authenticity and excellence could look like and be aware of the opportunities you have each day to create that life.

Realize that being authentic will attract excellence in your business and more business will be drawn to you as a result. Accept the search for your true self as ongoing progress that continues each day with new discoveries unfolding.

Living authentically is a way of life. It is a perception of the world around you and your place in it. How will your authenticity make a difference to yourself, your family and those around you each day? How will your authenticity and excellence leave the world a better place? By exploring who you truly are, you can find the answers to these questions. You can be proud of the contributions you leave behind and know that your best self has served the world.

Special *Woman Entrepreneur Extraordinaire* Offer

My gift to you is a free session to identify your values, goals and priorities to help you shine as an entrepreneur. Send a request for your 30-minute session to lisa@lisasinkiewicz.com. I am looking forward to hearing from you!

LISA CENTAMORE SINKIEWICZ
Speaker, Author, Educator Mentor,
Tastefully Simple, Inc.

Dream It! Believe It! Work It!

(508) 982-3678
lisa@lisasinkiewicz.com
www.lisasinkiewicz.com

Lisa Sinkiewicz believes you have the opportunity to be your authentic self as an entrepreneur and reflecting your values in your business truly allows you to shine. Lisa's approach stems from her own passion. She challenges you to dream big and pursue the action steps necessary to realize your own excellence and joy!

Through her experiences as an educator, direct sales industry top achiever, mom, speaker and trainer, Lisa has followed her heart's intuition to believe in and create the life of her dreams. Her desire to build her own legacy has helped inspire many to discover who they truly are and to explore their own aspirations. Lisa recognizes that entrepreneurial excellence results when her clients embrace their potential—she thrives on empowering her clients to transform their dreams into reality. Her energy engages her audiences and inspires them to be their best self and go beyond what is thought to be possible.

Lisa has earned top sales, recruiting and leadership recognition within her direct sales company and lives as an example to her children, Colin and Carly. She enjoys spending her free time with them and her husband, Jay.

From the Corporate World to Your Own World

Five Steps to Work that Gets You Out of Bed

By LaNette Parker, ACC, CEC

*P*icture waking up Monday morning. You rub the sleep out of your eyes and feel a familiar dread crawl over you at the thought of responding to your buzzing PDA. All those things you really want—moving from the corporate box into a life on your terms, creating your own schedule, tending to an overflowing bank account—feel so far off, almost impossible. After all, you have bills to pay. You do not want to upset the fragile apple cart of your family dynamics. It is better to sacrifice than to put yourself first *and* [fill in the blank here for whatever you tell yourself].

Time and again, women just like you wake up to this scenario. We consistently ask ourselves when it will be *our* turn. Why must we keep on keeping on? When/why, when/why, when/why—until we reel, dizzy from it all.

The toll this takes on us as individuals and as women adds up.

The toll it takes on the broader economy adds up, too. According to *The Economic Impact of Women-Owned Businesses in the United States*, a 2009 report from The Center for Women's Business Research, "If US-based, women-owned businesses were their own country, they would have the fifth largest GDP [Gross Domestic

Product] in the world, trailing closely behind Germany and ahead of countries including France, United Kingdom and Italy."

Consider what would have happened if Mary Kay Ash had never taken charge of her life to develop the Mary Kay® cosmetics company. Not only did she help women enhance their beauty, she also gave women a means of supporting themselves and each other. There are many success stories out there like hers—and yours can be one of them.

You owe it to yourself and others to live the greatest life you can imagine. When you hold back what you are here to contribute, you are not fulfilled, your family is not happy, your colleagues are not experiencing the fully-present you, your community is missing something—and the list goes on. Instead of focusing on what is not going well, turn your focus to what you can do. (See "From Passion to Success" by Simone Hoa on page 25.)

"We fall forward to succeed."
—Mary Kay Ash, American founder of Mary Kay Inc.®

Step One: Figure Out Your Offering

What do you have to offer? Start by answering the multi-million dollar question: If you won a multi-million dollar lottery, what would you do? What difference would you want to make in the world?

You may have an idea for a product. As you go about your everyday life, consider what would make your life more convenient, what "if-only" kinds of things your friends wish for, what product has already changed your life and you want to share with others.

You may have an idea for a service. Consider what draws people to you. Is it the way you express yourself in writing or art or through song? Is it the results people realize after talking with you? What pain have you experienced and overcome in your life that inspires others?

When you consider bringing either a product or service into the world, think big. Think really big. Answer these questions:

• What does success look like?

• Whom are you influencing?

• What are the results you want to achieve in others' lives?

• How does your physical environment—your relationships, your bank account, the beautiful things surrounding you—change as a result?

Now that you have some idea of your offering and how big a difference you can make, start building the bridge from where you are now to where you want to be.

> *"People will forget what you said*
> *People will forget what you did*
> *But people will never forget how you made them feel."*
> —Maya Angelou, African-American poet and author

Conduct research. Find other similar products and services on the market and determine what makes you unique. Rather than open another cupcake shop, consider your audience and the ambience you want to create. For example, an associate of mine is establishing a bakery as an evening destination. She is planning a place of community where adults can share a glass of wine while children have dessert. A holistic healer in my professional circle sets herself apart with her credentials and commitment to ongoing education that she happily shares with her clients.

Form partnerships. You are not alone. Most people love to support others and to be asked for help. You likely know people who know people who can provide tips and resources to help you set up a business, such as experts in branding, marketing, accounting and so on. Consider forming partnerships where you cross-refer clients. For example, you may be a freelance writer who refers clients to a graphic designer you trust for professional design help. Your graphic design partner may refer clients to you for writing support.

Know your value. Ask yourself what you would be willing to pay for your particular product or service, especially if you knew what a difference it could make in your life. Review competitors' pricing. Consider how you can package what you offer in an attractive way. Do not undervalue yourself and your offering. *You are worth it.*

Action Step: Get Started Now

Find a dry-erase marker. Go to a mirror you use every day. Look yourself in the eye and write three things on the mirror you absolutely want to have in your life. For example, "I am influencing millions with my spoken and written words of truth," or "I have a full calendar of paying clients."

Put this book down. Go do it now.

Stand in front of the mirror and read your statements aloud every day. As time goes by, and you gain clarity, you can use an eraser to remove the dry-erase ink and revise your statements.

Step Two: Make Your Plan

It is time to put a plan in place. If the word *plan* makes you squeamish, use *milestones.* This is your way of plotting the key steps that keep you focused and moving—that intentionally attract your next opportunity.

This document might be a step-by-step plan or a vision board, where you collect clippings of magazine pictures or articles that represent your milestones. For example, if you want to have a book published, you could create a vision board with photos of authors you admire, book covers and bookstores.

Use whatever media works for you. If you are highly creative, you may want to develop a video you can watch frequently to reinforce your confidence and your next steps.

As you consider your plan to transition from your paycheck job to your own business, keep these ideas in mind. (See "Think Like a CEO" by Alice Hinckley on page 37.)

It is not about the money. That sounds counterintuitive, doesn't it? Most people stay in unsatisfying jobs because they fear the loss of regular paychecks. The reasons for staying stuck are endless. What really keeps people from making the transition are self-sabotaging thoughts. The false belief that you do not have what it takes to build your business and out-earn the paycheck you have today. Once you can turn "I am not enough" into "I can be fabulously wealthy because I am greater than this," you will free yourself to move forward.

Consider what you will miss. Your paycheck job is more than a paycheck—although you may not always feel that way. Your job may give you a sense of community and purpose. Acknowledge those feelings and determine how you will bring these into your life once you transition to owning your business. For example, to ensure community, you can start or join a professional group of women business owners.

Be mindful of your time. What do you want your day to look like as you develop your business? You can easily be sucked in to the work of staying home to build your business, rather than leaving the house to call on potential clients. Attend events where you meet others, share information and follow up with the people you meet. This will be one of the most important uses of your time. Growing your contacts means more people are talking about you, more people are interested in what you offer, and, ultimately, you have more money in your pocket. One woman I know built her business by attending formal networking events and overcame a lifelong fear of public speaking to do so.

> *"Spend more time working on your business*
> *than working in your business."*
> —Caterina Rando, American speaker, author, publisher

Take action every day. Take one action every day to build your business. Remember, you are creating opportunities for yourself and others.

Action Step: Forty-five Minutes of Your Time

Clarify your long-term vision and bring it closer to home. The more specific you can be about what you want in the future, the more direct your route will be as you begin to take steps over the next few months to get you there.

Spend fifteen minutes answering each of these questions:

• What do you want your life to look like in two years?

• In one year?

• In six months?

Step Three: Improve Your Skills

We often expect too much of ourselves. Your road from the corporate world to owning and growing your business presents many opportunities for self-awareness. You will learn where you outshine everyone else, and what you wish you could do just a little better.

In my work with clients, time and again I see a core set of skills women entrepreneurs need to master as they move forward.

Communication. From self-talk to business communications, how you express your thoughts and ideas helps others know more about you and what you offer. More importantly than what you express, though, is how you listen and respond to others, especially when you hear news that makes you uncomfortable. When potential clients turn down your product or service, rather than sink into rejection, use the opportunity to say thank you and ask if they know of others who might be interested. This keeps the lines of communication open and shows confidence and maturity.

Relationship building. Connecting others to what they are looking for is the simplest way of building relationships. If you come across something, such as an article, product or service, that you think someone might be interested in seeing, let them know about it. Also, practice good relationship habits. When you say you will get back to someone, follow up within 24 hours, even if only to provide a status update. Building relationships takes time and care. (See "It's Not Stalking...It's Follow Up!" by Elizabeth McCormick on page 143.)

Business management. Having worked in the corporate world, you have a leg up on those who do not have that kind of experience. You know how the flow of business works from getting and keeping clients to paying the bills and rewarding others for creating a profit.

What more you need to know about business management comes down to the details, such as keeping business and personal accounts separate, tracking expenses and revenue and investing in people and products that will give you a return on that investment. (See "The Ten Commandments of Small Business Success" by Nancy Lewellen on page 61.)

Training, mentoring, coaching. Invest in yourself and your excellence. Determine what additional training can improve your offering. Ask someone you admire to serve as your mentor. Consider working with a coach to keep you inspired and focused on your business and personal goals.

Action Step: Your Skill-Building To-Do List

Read this book with pen and paper in hand and make a to-do list of every tool and tip you think will help you and every action you need to take. Start now with this chapter.

Step Four: Get Moving

Making change in your life, especially taking a leap of faith and creating work that gets you out of bed every day, is not for the faint of heart. You have what it takes, you have an offering, you have a plan, you have a skill set, and you are uniquely you.

Say "yes" to the gift of you. You can create whatever life you want, whatever relationships you want, whatever income level you want. Invite yourself to the table and to a new way of working.

Ask yourself the tough questions. What is keeping you where you are? Complete this sentence, "I am stuck because I am allowing myself to [fill in the blank]." When you answer this question, you connect with your truth and begin to own your circumstances.

When you own your circumstances, the mountains in front of you soften into rolling hills.

Be willing to let go. Once you have identified what is holding you back, say goodbye and create space for the life you want. Often, the very thing you think you must have is the first thing to go. In the case of relationships and jobs, people feel trapped due to loyalty or responsibility. What do you feel when you consider letting go? Most people experience a sense of freedom and possibility. Honor your intuition since it is your guide.

Action Step: Put One Foot Forward

Consider what holds you back. Is it relationships, habits, material desires? Of the things that come to mind, what holds you back the most? If you could change just one thing, what would that be?

What is one step you can take in the next 24 hours to move away from what is keeping you where you are and move you to the life you want?

Step Five: Master Your Mind

Fear and doubt have a way of creeping in just when you feel a surge of triumph. Why is this? You are changing and evolving, moving into your own. You are shedding old ways to become who you are. With growth and change come the naysayers—from messages hardwired into your mind from long ago or from a comment someone made yesterday that sent you off track.

Stay strong in your truth. When fear arises, because it will, remember your most confident days. Remember what you are here on this earth to do. Remember the difference you are making and how you have influenced others. There is more for you to do.

Have a response to "I can't." When I asked a client how she could go about moving toward the ideal life she wanted, she said it was not likely, then added, "Let's assume I can."

A lightbulb went on and "let's assume I can" became her mantra. Assume that *you* can, too. When you do, you will overcome the voices—real or imagined—who tell you otherwise.

Surround yourself with successful people. Find people you admire, observe their outlook on life and take note of their habits. Adopt the behaviors and attitudes that make sense for you and make them your own. Acting as if you are already successful carries you into the league you wish to join.

Action Step: Appreciate the Journey

Stand in front of the mirror you used in the "Get Started Now" action of Step 1. See your beauty. Appreciate that you are on a journey.

Look yourself in your eyes. Allow yourself to believe.

Believe.

You are worth it.

Now What? Keep Moving!

Picture waking up Monday morning. You rub the sleep out of your eyes and picture the day ahead. All those things you really want— taking care of your body at the gym, having energy throughout the day, sharing your soul with clients, family and friends—are right here, today. You attract people with your knowledge and confidence. You surround yourself with beauty. Your bank account reflects your inner wealth.

You have made it. You have taken the steps to free yourself and create a role for yourself in a world that is uniquely you. You find that as life unfolds in front of you, you experience greater opportunities to give to others. Ideas flow in about what is next for you. You keep believing. You keep moving.

It is up to you.

Special *Woman Entrepreneur Extraordinaire* Offer

Live YOUR life. Grow your self-worth and net worth. Enroll in my "It's Your Turn for a Change" coaching program and receive a 15-percent discount. This program includes 24, empower-packed, 45-minute sessions, unlimited email support and newsletter subscription. Email lanette@lanetteparker.com or call (415) 317-3371 to take advantage of this offer today.

LANETTE PARKER, ACC, CEC

You are worth the greatest life you can imagine

(415) 317-3371
lanette@lanetteparker.com
www.lanetteparker.com

A passion for abundant living, a genuine interest in people and an uncommon ability to move others to achieve great success are the hallmark of LaNette's life. She brings a lifetime of character-building experiences to her heart-centered executive and life coaching and communication consulting practice. She overcame massive debt to create a six-figure net worth by working through career confusion to owning her own business. She found her soul mate after years of unhealthy relationships, and she lost 100 pounds and has kept it off!

LaNette developed the *It's Your Turn for a Change* coaching program to inspire individuals, and she serves as a Motivation Factor® certified partner, engaging and motivating teams to realize common goals. She is one of 4,000 coaches worldwide with the International Coach Federation's prestigious credential.

LaNette honed her business intuition and creativity working with some of the world's most renowned companies over the course of fifteen years in human resources and communication consulting. She is a contributing author to the Amazon.com® top-ten bestseller *Empowering Transformations for Women,* published by Power You Publishing in 2011, and one of 6,000 global collaborators on The Difference Project, an international movement aimed at opening humanity's heart.

From Passion to Success
Secrets for Making Money Doing What You Love
By Simone Hoa

What is passion, and how do we look at passion? It is a burning desire anxiously waiting to be liberated, to express itself through the activities we do, to guide us to do what we love, to get the maximum enjoyment, satisfaction and happiness from what we do and from life. Passion provides us with the necessary fuel and drive to pursue our dreams.

What about success? I do not believe success is measured in terms of money or material wealth. It is measured by the way you live your life—doing what you love. Passion and success go hand in hand, and you can have a business and a life filled with both!

The primordial ingredient to the success recipe is *passion.* It is the root of all success and fulfilled dreams. If we look at the lives of successful people, their success is attributed to their passion for what they did and how they lived their lives. When you live your true passion, your potential is released from your deep, fertile mind, so you can achieve truly significant success.

Passion is the first and foremost component of success. However, it is not always obvious what our passion is. I am going to share how I came to discover my passion, and how, from my own experience, I created the 5A-Process to help people who are serious about discovering their passion make changes in their life to pursue their dream.

"It [passion] is an all-consuming feeling that keeps you awake at night with your brain swimming with ideas and dreams."
—Gary Vaynerchuk, Belarusian social entrepreneur
and bestselling author

Let's step back to the year 2004 when I suffered a financial loss of more than $100,000. I had lost a court case and found myself without any financial support. I had to close my company.

I felt powerless. It took me almost five years to reconnect with myself, re-define my identity and start to rebuild. During this time, I devoured personal development books, listened and learned from CDs and attended seminars. Then, on December 20th, 2008, after suffering yet another blow to my self-esteem, I vowed I would never let my self-esteem be hurt again.

After taking a Dale Carnegie® course and joining Toastmasters International®, I made the decision to pursue a career in public speaking. I discovered my new, *true* passion and life purpose—to help people of all ages around the world to discover their passion and live it to the fullest in order to achieve success in their personal and professional life—as early as possible!

I am a Vietnamese woman in the sunset of my life, and I became an inspirational speaker in a foreign country, delivering speeches in French and English. I am not afraid to fail and will never give up because my new passion is true and unstoppable.

The 5A-Process—Your Shortcut to Success

During my nearly five years of self-discovery, I went through a painful and lengthy process to discover my true passion. I came to realize the extraordinary power of passion in successful people's lives, and I decided to write and record what was happening to me. My desire is to share it with you to help you achieve the same result in a much shorter time. I call it the 5A-Process because it takes five steps that start with the letter A:

- Awareness

- Analysis

- Acceptance

- Attitude

- Action

If you use my 5A-Process, you will discover your passion and take action to pursue it, just as I did. You will be able to do so in a matter of weeks or, at the most, a few months—not the years it took me!

Briefly, what does each step involve?

Awareness. This is being conscious of who you are at this stage in your life, including your identity, values, priorities, beliefs, likes, dislikes, physical and financial health, relationships and so on. It is the process of identifying the real, authentic you. It is not the old you anymore as the old you has not served you. Past limiting beliefs have held you back and prevented you from being bold enough to act on new opportunities. To release self-imposed limitations, you have to identify their sources—they can come from your family, in particular your parents, your teachers, friends and professional colleagues who exert strong influences on you. (See "Master the Secrets for Entrepreneurial Success" by Beverly Lenz on page 49.)

When you are successful in determining the new authentic you, you need to surround yourself with a new environment of positive and optimistic-minded people who will share your vision and ideas, support your commitment and help you achieve your dreams.

This first step of awareness has helped me redefine my identity and priorities that dictate the way I relate to my new environment and change habits to consciously respect my authenticity and self-discovery.

Analysis. Now, analyze your strengths, weaknesses, qualities, faults, talents and skills based on your values and priorities. This begins connecting your strengths and talents with what you would enjoy doing every day to make a living. When you realize what you are good at, you start to feel your passion or feel again repressed passion. You feel strong emotions, such as enthusiasm and excitement, when you talk about what you like to do. This creates confidence and trust from your audience, which in turn, instills more self-confidence. You start believing strongly in your newly discovered passion. (See "Rapid Business Growth for Financial Freedom" by Arlene Krantz on page 85.)

As mentioned earlier, my experience with Dale Carnegie and Toastmasters International confirmed my new passion in public speaking. I "saw" myself on stage speaking like the guests speakers I had listened to. My new passion was born, and I decided to become a public speaker within weeks of its discovery.

Acceptance. After completing the first two steps, you now have realized consciously who you are with your strengths and weaknesses. Realizing is one thing— fully accepting it is another. This acceptance step requires an attitude of 100 percent personal responsibility for your actions. You must accept the consequences of your actions and understand their impact on those around you. To be able to assume this complete responsibility, you need to have control over your emotions and reactions and gain control over your internal world as much as possible. The concept that helps us to practice this attitude can be summarized in the following formula:

$$E + R = O$$

Event + Reaction = Outcome

My typical recovery situation after the huge financial loss illustrates perfectly this personal responsibility concept. I used to blame my ex-partner for my disastrous situation. However, blaming did not bring anything good to me. On the contrary, it delayed my recovery. I decided to take responsibility for my naïve belief and unfortunate mistake and use that lesson for future business. This kind of thinking brings us to the next step of the 5A-Process.

Attitude. Have you heard, "Change your attitude, and you can change your life?" This concept has stood the test of time. Change your attitude today, at this instant, and you can change your life today, at this instant.

Since attitude is the starting point to effect change, the sooner you change your attitude and adopt a better one, the sooner you can start making a change in your life—for the better. A conscious change of attitude results in a conscious change of habits and behavior. As behavior changes, your life and the world around you start to change. This is the beginning of the new you. Your new passion influences the way you think and the way you act. It makes you feel alive.

Action. The achievement of the four steps above will not lead to real results unless the fifth "A" is activated. Taking action is the key to pursuing your passion and dreams. It initiates movement in the direction you want to follow and the path you have chosen to take. You can start changing your life by making different choices that will initiate different actions and bring about different results.

The practice of the 5A-Process is the reason I evolved from the emotionally desperate state I experienced and could face the huge challenge I had to overcome to become the person I am today. If I can do it as an immigrant, you can do it, too.

Make Money from Your Passion

It is fine and dandy to want to pursue one's passion— the challenge is to find ways to not only make a living from it, but to actually prosper with it by exploiting it smartly to the fullest. Briefly, the two basic, yet most necessary ingredients to business success are vision and strategy. (See "Exemplifying Authenticity and Excellence as an Entrepreneur" by Lisa Centamore Sinkiewicz on page 1.)

Once your vision is shaped, the next crucial step is to devise your strategy. No matter how clear your vision is, if you do not have a smart strategy to implement, you will not achieve the results you want.

After your vision and strategy are in place, you can begin making money doing what you love! Here are eight powerful steps to help you.

Step One: The Power of Branding

One of the secrets of business success lies in the creation of a powerful unique brand. (See "Communicating Your Personal Brand" by Melanie Fitzpatrick on page 107.)

What *you* think about your brand does not matter. What matters is what *others* think about it. Define your brand clearly, so it stands out in the minds of your ideal clients and reflects your uniqueness, which is comprised of your skills, talents, personality, life experiences and gifts. This is not enough, however. You need to weave it consistently into your marketing strategy to generate potentially unlimited success in your business.

Establishing your brand is an equally important key to your success. Communicate it through visual branding by putting a "face" on your company, products and services. This stamps it with your personal identity and creates a living brand across all media, such as promotional products (business cards, brochures, press kit and so on), your website and all social media.

Step Two: The Power of Web Marketing

All entrepreneurs need to leverage technology to speed the growth and success of their business with tools such as emails, video marketing, blogging, newsletters, teleseminars, webinars, web sites, social media and so on. With the fast, unstoppable growth of technology available at our fingertips, you must take advantage of it, or you will be left behind.

What are you currently doing to maximize your web marketing? Are your social media profiles current and market oriented? If not, set some time on your calendar to make it happen!

Step Three: The Power of Direct and Written Marketing

To reach your market effectively, choose specific strategies to achieve specific results. Consider face-to-face networking, public speaking, workshops, radio shows, trade shows, sponsorships, authorship, articles and so on. Your choice is based on your strengths, talents and skills. Your strengths and uniqueness will help you develop appropriate and pertinent marketing tools to suit your target market and speed the growth of your business. I chose to use my talent in public speaking at the beginning of my career as a marketing strategy to create credibility and visibility quickly. I then developed coaching services and workshops to complement my speaking. I built my business to the point where I won the 2010 Best Growth trophy from the Boomers Entrepreneurs Association only six months into my business.

Step Four: The Power of Customer Service

How do you create the *wow* effect? Customer service can make or break a business, and it is an art to cultivate. How do you stand out? By creating more *wow* effects than your competition.

What is a *wow* effect? It is the art of surprising the client with a service that offers more value than expected and delivers more than what was promised. Will your clients be loyal to you and refer new clients to you? Absolutely! (See "Customer Service Cuts through Competition" by Sheri Brunnquell on page 131 for information on how to use the web for customer service.)

What can you do to create the *wow* factor for your clients?

Step Five: The Power of Public Speaking

I am a testament to the value of this market for creating exponential growth for your business. Public speaking helps to generate credibility and increase visibility, so you can leverage your entrepreneurial power. For me, this skill is one of the most important in business leveraging. (See "Become a Sought After Speaker and Make Your Business Thrive!" by Caterina Rando on page 221.)

Do you do public speaking now? If not, what topics are you passionate about that you could present to an audience of potential clients?

If you are afraid of speaking in public, check out Toastmasters International or other sources of speaking training. You cannot afford to ignore this means of growing your business.

Step Six: The Power of Focus

This power is often neglected or misunderstood and under-appreciated. Many entrepreneurs do not focus on their strengths and brand. Instead, their focus is divided among several services or products they offer. In doing this, the power of focus is lost. You cannot grow your business if you do not leverage the power of focus—it is that simple.

How do you regain focus in your business? Concentrate on your strengths and expertise. The more you focus on these two elements, the faster you will grow your business and the more success you will achieve.

Step Seven: The Power of Expertise and Excellence

How do you become known as *the expert* in what you do? Your brand and your pursuit of excellence make you stand out from the crowd. Why do clients decide to do business with you rather than your competitors? It is what you are *known for* that contributes to your success.

Clients seek the best products and services they can get at a price that fits their perceived value of the product or service they like to buy. Sharpen your skills, be the best you can be in what you do, and clients will seek you out rather than you seeking them.

Your passion, expertise and excellence are your best and most powerful influence tools to attract your ideal clients. Exploit the "know, like and trust" factors to grow your business.

Step Eight: The Power of Leverage

Any entrepreneur who is not exploiting this power is missing the boat completely. Leverage is creating a massive result with a minimum of effort. You can create leverage when your business and action are based on your passion, strengths and skills.

The more leverage you have in your business, the better chance you will have of achieving huge success. My business success is leveraged on my talent in public speaking, which in turn generates income streams from seminars, workshops and group coaching. I also leverage my writing skills with the co-authorship of three books and my own soon-to-be-released book *Success Has No Age: You Are Never Too Young or Too Old to Live Your Passion.*

Different entrepreneurs have different strengths and skills. Use them smartly to exploit maximum leverage in your business and speed its growth exponentially.

In conclusion, there is no one secret for making money doing what you love. It takes a lot of hard work, combined with smart strategies to prosper with your passion. However, for me, the vital role of passion remains the critical ingredient to the success recipe. Without passion, there will be no energy, force or drive to muster the necessary courage and confidence you need to pursue your dream and keep up momentum and enthusiasm in the face of obstacles and difficulties.

> *"The journey of a thousand miles starts with the first step."*
> —Lao Tzu, Chinese philosopher

The pleasure and joy of success is not the destination. The joy comes from the process of becoming the person you have to become to achieve success.

Set goals that will make you the kind of person you need to be to succeed. I have applied this concept from the beginning of my new, challenging career and have already reaped numerous success results in a short time. These fast and concrete results are the product of the secrets described in this chapter.

If you want to make money doing what you love, discover and live your true passion, potential and life purpose. Achieve personal and financial success and live the life of your dreams as you have envisioned them.

Special *Woman Entrepreneur Extraordinaire* Offer

My *free gift* to you is thirty minutes of coaching by telephone! Just go to my web site and register with the special code: WEE. When you sign up, you will also receive free "The Power of Courage," a chapter from my book *Roadmap to Success*, from Insight Publishing in 2009.

SIMONE HOA
Passion 2 Success

(541) 777-9785
s.aubrey@passion2success.com
www.passion2success.com
www.passion2successgift.com

Simone Hoa is Vietnamese and proud to be a social entrepreneur with a career in inspirational public speaking and coaching in personal and business development. She shows her clients and audiences how to live their passion and achieve success in life.

Simone's services include public conferences, seminars, workshops, corporate keynotes and one-on-one and group coaching. Her life mission is to help people discover their passion, create their vision and live a successful lifestyle with total freedom. Her mantra is, "Success is not a struggle. It's a lifestyle." She believes people can be happy doing what they love every day and achieve financial success at the same time. Simone is the author of *"Success Has No Age: You Are Never Too Young or Too Old to Live Your Passion."*

A businesswoman in Montreal, Quebec, Simone has a strong background in business and marketing that she combines with her current career as a speaker and coach in personal and business development. She is known for her inspirational speeches and her guaranteed, fast and concrete results in coaching.

Think Like a CEO

Creating Lightbulb Moments™ for Business Success

By Alice Hinckley, CPA

With the fast pace of business today, it is vital that you think like a CEO if your desired outcome is to earn like a CEO. What does it take to think like a CEO? There are four areas of focus all business owners must consider on a consistent basis to be successful. As you review the various topics, take time to search for your "lightbulb" moments when an idea piques your interest or creates excitement for the results that idea may create in your business.

Some of the points will be familiar to you. Other ideas will be brand new. At least once or twice, the light will go on for you. Discover the one or two actions you can implement immediately that will positively change the trajectory of your business forever. Decide to put one or two of these items into action for the next thirty days. If you try to do everything at once, you may feel overwhelmed or find that you have no focus. Instead, concentrate on improving the areas you identify and commit to taking action in those areas. This step will create success for you. In any business endeavor, consistent action is the key.

So what is a CEO? A chief executive officer has ultimate responsibility for overseeing the success of a business endeavor. Whether you are a new entrepreneur or a seasoned business owner, evaluating four areas of responsibility will create insights for growth. CEOs work diligently to make decisions from the facts first, not their emotions. Make a concerted effort to evaluate decisions in your business like a CEO in these areas:

- Managing your finances
- Managing yourself
- Managing your time
- Managing your team

Manage Your Finances: Return on Investment

Do you keep good financial records and know how to read and evaluate those records? Many small business owners make mistakes that CEOs do not because CEOs regularly review and update financial records. As a wise CEO, you need to track income and expenses at least weekly, so schedule time on your calendar to review your financial status. What areas are producing the most income? How can you capitalize on those income streams? Are any expenses high in proportion to the return? Where are you relative to your annual budget?

Do these questions make you uncomfortable? Find an expert, such as a certified public accountant, or take a class at the local community college on reviewing financial statements. Create confidence in your ability to make informed business decisions from the records you keep. You gain an added bonus when income tax time comes around each year—your financial information is organized and the process of preparing your returns is simplified. (See "The Ten Commandments of Small Business Success" by Nancy Lewellen on page 61.)

Do you properly allocate earnings from your business? All financial experts share a common theme, "Pay Yourself First." In his book *The Richest Man in Babylon,* re-issued by Signet in 2004, George S. Clason shared his advice for wisely managing finances. Every time you receive income from your business, commit to paying yourself first.

- Take the first ten percent and move the funds to a separate savings account.

- Next, donate ten percent to your church, favorite charity or community. Successful people give back repeatedly. This is called the *Law of Sowing and Reaping.*

- Now, invest ten percent back into your business for advertising, as a bonus to a valuable employee or contractor, or to attend an event or seminar that will help you grow personally and professionally.

- Operate your business on the remaining seventy percent of income.

Take time to evaluate where you waste money. Some people have trouble with this concept. Do you still pay monthly for marketing on a website that has not produced business in months? Even if the cost is minimal, make sure you are getting results from the money you spend. If you pay $25 a month, that totals $300 a year.

Consistently evaluate small expenses, so your funds can be used to create the most income. Think like a CEO—make small sacrifices that turn into large dividends. Be sharp and control small, wasteful spending.

Do you invest in your business image like a CEO? Invest in your promotional materials. You want them to be impressive and memorable and represent you as an established business owner. Do not skimp during development of your logo, branding, website and business cards. Go top notch. You do not have to spend a fortune— just invest wisely to create your brand. Ask other business owners whom you respect and admire for referrals to ensure your funds reap the most polished products to promote your business.

Do you invest in networking like a CEO? Have business cards and promotional materials with you at all times. Gather contact information from people to whom you give materials, so you can follow up in a timely manner. (See "It's Not Stalking...It's Follow Up!" by Elizabeth McCormick on page 143.)

Get involved and use the power of belonging to a large group to help leverage your business success. Having a presence at your local chamber of commerce also brings exemplary exposure to your business.

Make sure you *get involved* in the organizations. When you create long-term relationships, your dues to these organizations are investments in creating income. If you do not become active in the organization, you are just creating an expense that has no return.

Manage Yourself: Setting and Communicating Goals

Who must you become to earn like a CEO? Most business owners set goals and focus solely on the accomplishment of a dollar number related to sales, income and so on. The real question you must ask yourself is, Who must you become *within yourself* to reach those goals? What skills or character traits do you need to improve on in order to think and earn like a CEO? This can include listening, writing, communicating, marketing, speaking, strategic planning, positive outlook, goal setting, focus, improved attitude, discipline, consistency and so on.

> *"Most people live and die with their music still unplayed. They never dare to try."*
> —Mary Kay Ash, American, founder Mary Kay®

Personal growth is the key to improving or developing in any area. Turn your car into a classroom and listen to books or a motivational series instead of music. One of my favorite possessions is my library card. It is a free pass to books and CDs that help you learn more about your strengths and strengthen areas that are weaker.

Ask your mentor and other business people you admire to name their favorite personal development book, speaker or author. Make sure you become more of the person you want to be each day.

There is a compound effect to personal growth. If you decide to read or listen to inspirational or educational materials fifteen minutes a day, six days a week, in just one month, you will have invested 360 minutes, or six hours, in your personal and professional development. In a year's time, you will have fed 72 hours of positive information into your system. Talk about becoming the person who can achieve your goals!

Do you confidently set compelling goals? Having a formula for your goals will create the power of momentum. Here is a positive formula for goal setting:

On or before (date) I am (what you want to achieve) because (why you want to achieve it). I will become a person who (characteristic to develop) because of striving for my outcome.

For example, your goal may be to increase your personal sales by ten percent. Your compelling goal might read like this:

On or before September 1, I am consistently contacting one additional prospect each day to create a ten percent or more increase in my income because I want my spouse to be able to stop working his part-time job and have more time together as a family. I will become a person who embraces family moments, feels proud for working hard to reach goals and gives a special gift to my spouse because of striving for my outcome.

Creating a visual anchor makes your goal more real and consistently reminds you to take action. Treasure maps are a colorful and motivating way to keep your goals right in front of you. Cut out pictures and words that represent your goal from magazines. Paste them onto a poster board or put them in a small photo book you can carry with you. Display the treasure map where you will see it during the day.

An outstanding example of the results of creating a treasure map is my husband, Bob. Bob has been an avid golfer for years, yet with all the rounds of golf he has played, he has never landed a hole-in-one. Recently, we created our annual treasure maps, and Bob included a picture of a group of men playing golf with the words "hole-in-one" next to the picture. A few months later, we vacationed with several friends, and Bob got his first hole-in-one surrounded by people he loved.

Write your goal on index cards. Keep one with you at all times, one by the bed and one on your desk. Top income earners in our country review goals daily. The best of the best read their goals at least twice a day. Improve your life with these small, simple disciplines, so you can think and earn like a CEO.

Manage Your Time: Establishing and Following a System

Do you consider time to be your most valuable resource? Each day contains exactly 24 hours. The activities you choose to fill those hours determine whether your life will be mediocre or exceptional. Do you have a system to aid in prioritizing activities, so the most important tasks are completed effectively and efficiently? Do you recognize time wasters and implement systems to streamline time associated with less crucial activities? Master your time and watch your business grow exponentially while you feel less burdened or overwhelmed.

CEOs are proactive, not reactive. You could not successfully build a house without a detailed set of blueprints, and you cannot have a productive day without a plan of action. One highly effective tool is to take ten minutes at the end of each day to plan the following day. Make a list of tasks that must be accomplished and then prioritize each task. Put an "A" next to the must-do items. Put a "B" beside items you ought to complete, and a "C" next to items that are not vital to be completed that day. Next, take each group, A's, B's and C's, and rank the items in each group in order of importance.

Commit to getting the A items done before anything else on your list. Do not be tempted to complete B or C items first, just so you can mark something off your list. Think like a CEO—be disciplined and complete first the tasks that have the most positive impact on your business.

What activities steal the most time out of your day? It is important to have flexibility for important items that arise during your business day. It is also vital to control tasks that "steal" your most precious resource—your time. CEOs actively manage their time for optimum results. Here are some ideas for streamlining in three areas that can quickly sideline your results.

Email. Set aside specific time during the day to read and return emails. One day a week, actively unsubscribe to unnecessary items that fill your inbox. Turn off the sounds on your computer or PDA informing you an email has arrived, so you are not tempted to stop and check the message. Remember this master key to productivity: *Touch it once!* When you read an email, respond immediately and file it away.

Phone calls. Block out a time in the morning and the afternoon to return phone calls and initiate contact with prospects, clients or team members. You can even set proper expectations by specifying these times in your voicemail with a message that includes something like this, "I will be returning calls between 10 a.m. and 11 a.m. and 2 p.m. and 3 p.m. today."

Interruptions. Manage how often you are interrupted by setting expectations with those around you. According to W. Todd Smith in *Little Things Matter,* published in 2010 by Success Books, every time you are interrupted during a task, it can take up to ten minutes to refocus and get back to where you were before the distraction. Close your door. Do not answer unscheduled calls unless it is an emergency. Allow yourself the quiet focused time necessary to complete a high-importance task.

Maximize your effectiveness by managing your time like a CEO. Be strong enough to set boundaries for yourself and others. Continually evaluate ways to upgrade the quality of the time you invest in each task.

Manage Your Team: Leading Others

Are you leading with integrity and respect? People want to be around excited people who show interest in them, are respectful and have integrity. CEOs have a strong belief in themselves, in their company and in their team. Surround yourself with positive people. It is widely accepted that you become a combination of the five people you spend the most time with in your life. Think about that. Make sure the people with whom you invest the most time have character traits you want to develop. Choose to be an example by your own admirable character traits, so you have strong influence for the better on people around you.

Do you know the goals of your team members? Having company goals and working toward them as a team is crucial. However, your team is made up of individuals who have their own personal and professional goals. Connect with each person and make notes regarding their individual dreams. Knowing that you care will inspire them to reach for more, and you can remind them of their ultimate goals during difficult periods.

These same concepts apply to sole proprietors. Even if you do not have a large team of people working directly for you, a support team exists among your colleagues, suppliers and referral network. Do you know the goals of your web designer or attorney? When people know you care about their desires, they will feel much more connected to you and work harder to help your business succeed. Be authentic and sincere when asking about goals and promising to assist others to succeed in reaching theirs. CEOs engage all parties around them to be included in their team.

> *"A good objective of leadership is to help those who are doing poorly to do well and to help those who are doing well to do even better."*
> —Kim Kiyosaki, American entrepreneur, founder Rich Woman®

Have you mastered the skill of listening? Most CEOs listen respectfully and draw people closer with their rapt attention to the speaker. Demonstrate that you are interested in the person speaking by making eye contact, asking questions and not interrupting. Often, people are so busy deciding how they plan to respond to comments made in a conversation, they do not fully listen to what is being said. Be present and attentive. People really do not care how much you know until they know how much you care. Show care and respect by actively listening during conversations.

Powered-up Action Now!

What was your first "lightbulb" moment as you read this chapter? What actions will you take to implement this idea in your business in the next thirty days?

Being a CEO is a big job! You have made great strides in taking control of your own finances, freedom and choices by becoming an entrepreneur. Now, take the next step and become a CEO.

Choose to implement small action steps every day and start thinking like the CEO you are!

Special *Woman Entrepreneur Extraordinaire* Offer

Curious how effective you currently are as a CEO?

Visit www.YourLightbulbMoments.com and download your complimentary CEO Mindset Assessment, so you can evaluate yourself as of today and plan to improve your CEO mindset in the future.

ALICE HINCKLEY, CPA

Creating Lightbulb Moments™
for business success

(972) 335-2252
alice@yourlightbulbmoments.com
www.yourlightbulbmoments.com

Alice Hinckley, CPA, has been an entrepreneur since the early 1990s. In addition to establishing and managing a successful accounting business, Alice is a professional business strategist, author and sought-after speaker. Her passion is to help her clients grow their businesses and experience life more deeply through insightful coaching, informational presentations and high-level life experiences that include laughing, loving, sharing, growing and stretching every day.

Through her CEO Mindset Strategies, energetic presentations and direct selling teamwork, Alice helps others succeed in all areas of their lives. Using her background as a certified public accountant, she offers her clients a pragmatic approach for making life decisions that immediately serve them. Alice continues to expand her influence by attending personal development events and speaking to audiences of all sizes.

An avid tennis player, Alice enjoys traveling, reading, golf, entertaining and creating magic moments with friends and family. Giving back to the community is an integral part of her life, so she serves on the board of directors for many local charities near her home in Dallas, Texas. She lives with her incredible husband, Bob, and their two maltipoos, Allie and Baxter.

Master the Secrets for Entrepreneurial Success

Break Free from What's Holding You Back and Reclaim Your Power!

By Beverly Lenz, RN, MS

*I*once misplaced a favorite pen. I looked everywhere, including my purse. My husband started helping me.

"I'll look in your purse," he said.

"I already looked there," I replied. "It's not there."

He looked anyway, and there was my pen in the side pocket where I could have sworn I looked several times. Once I believed my pen was not in my purse, I could not see it.

Subconscious beliefs are powerful. They affect your ability to see and take advantage of opportunities. They affect your mood and your desire or reluctance to take risks. Ultimately, they affect how successful you will become. They stop you from trying and cause you to ignore critical connections for business growth because you cannot see past your subconscious beliefs.

According to cellular biologist Bruce H. Lipton in his book *The Biology of Belief,* published by Hay House in 2010, "Ninety-five percent of our beliefs are at the subconscious level."

You draw people and events to you based on your belief systems. These beliefs function like computer programs in the hard drive of your subconscious, creating sickness or health, wealth or poverty. They also form your perceptions of yourself, such as powerful or powerless, fearful or safe, worthy or worthless. This means that 95 percent of your business and life are being run by beliefs you are unaware of or cannot recognize!

You Are of Two Minds

You have only one mind. That mind possesses two distinct inter-dependent and characteristic parts—the conscious and subconscious. Think of the subconscious mind as the hard drive of your computer, storing data in the form of memories and experiences. Bruce H. Lipton maintains that every cell in the body is like a programmable computer chip. The subconscious mind tells the cells what to do, such as breathe, digest your meal and keep your heart beating. It also programs the cells with *tapes* derived from perceptions of events and situations. For example, let's say when you were seven years old, you tripped while out hiking and your friends made fun of you. As an adult, you now may view hiking as unpleasant.

The conscious mind, on the other hand, chooses and sets goals. Maybe you want to land a major contract with a large corporation. Any trauma stored in the subconscious may prevent you from taking action. A parent's voice telling you that you would never amount to anything keeps you from making connections with senior executives who have the power to give you a contract. A public reprimand from a teacher about a mistake on the blackboard may stop you from finishing the proposal to the company.

No matter how much your conscious mind wants to do something, subconscious beliefs can keep you trapped in old patterns and behaviors that sabotage your business and your life. By accessing your subconscious mind, you can free yourself from old scripts that undermine your self-confidence, your success, interpersonal relationships and prosperity. In this chapter, I will reveal six secrets to help you overcome limiting subconscious beliefs that stand in the way of your success.

Secret One: Identify Limiting Beliefs

Freedom from limiting beliefs starts by identifying them. Schedule time to identify beliefs that are sabotaging your business success, so you can address them later in the chapter. Keep a notebook at the ready to jot down beliefs that come to you as you read through the material.

Some limiting beliefs are created by negative self-talk. This is the critic inside your mind that convinces you to not go after what you want. It is the voice that tells you what you believe about yourself. You recognize it because it says things like:

• I can't.

• I'm too old or too young.

• It's too hard.

• I'm not smart enough or not good enough.

• I have to struggle to be successful.

• I'm at the mercy of the economy.

• I can't charge a lot because I'm not worth it.

• I'm a failure.

• I'm a loser.

If any of these statements are familiar, you are discovering your own negative beliefs. Take a few minutes and think about other negative statements you say to yourself. Jot them down.

Limiting beliefs around money. Success begets money. How much success your subconscious may allow you to have can be determined by your beliefs about money.

What did your parents believe about money? Did you hear statements like these:

• "Money doesn't grow on trees."

• "I have to work hard for every penny I get."

• "Money is the root of all evil."

• "The less money you have, the more God loves you."

• "There is never enough to go around."

Did your parents argue about money? If so, you may believe, "If I have money, I'll never be happy." Some common mis-beliefs are, "It's wrong to have more money than I need," or "It's wrong to have more money than my family or my friends have."

Keeping the money you make is often challenging due to beliefs that "If I have a lot of money, I'll lose it," or "If I have a lot of money, I'll have to give it away or people will think I'm selfish." The latter belief system brings up one of the primary reasons why boundaries with others are so important to being successful and having and keeping money. You have a choice to say "no" when people ask you for money.

Limiting beliefs around worthiness. Many people are unsuccessful at attaining what they want in business because they feel they do not deserve it. Deep-seated beliefs, such as "I'm bad," "I'm nothing," "I'm a mistake," "I'm unlovable," and others like these, determine if you feel worthy of success and abundance. If you believe you are undeserving, you will never be successful.

Worthiness issues can determine the exact amount of money you charge for your services, what you believe people are willing to pay and how much money you actually get. This can make or break your business. Low self-worth causes people to run their businesses like a hobby and wonder why they are just "getting by."

Limiting beliefs around fear of failure or fear of success. In my experience, many entrepreneurs fall into one of these two categories—fear of success or fear of failure. Remember, the job description of the subconscious is to keep you safe and alive. The subconscious might relate success to you being more visible.

What happened when you were "seen" as a child? Were you criticized? Punished? Attacked? Ridiculed? Bullied? The subconscious, in an effort to keep you safe, might sabotage your efforts to achieve success. (See "Break Free to Six Figures" by Georgina Sweeney on page 209.)

A limiting belief like, "If I am successful, I will be alone," may prevent you from realizing success since the outward signs of success might leave you open to judgment, jealousy and feelings of being unloved. Being alone is a primitive fear for most people, dating from prehistoric times when it was dangerous to be without your tribe. A part of your mind senses a threat to your survival and sabotages you to keep you safe and alive. Not exactly what you want as an entrepreneur.

Fear of failure comes from how we are perceived by others. For example, it may be safer to do nothing than to try and fail. This is one of the biggest belief systems behind procrastination along with "Do it perfectly or not at all."

You have now identified some of the beliefs you know you *do not* want. The next step is to know what you want.

Secret Two: Know What You Want

How do you create what you want in your life and work? You have to *know* what you want. Every goal is actually two goals: What you want *and* what you do not want. They are opposite sides of the same coin. Often, even when you believe you are thinking about something you want, you are actually thinking about the opposite!

What you think and what you get are always a vibrational match. Many clients have come to me and when I ask them what they want, they begin by telling me everything they do not want.

What do you *not* want? Make a list! Then turn all those things you do not want into what you *do* want. For example, change:

- "I don't want to be sick" to "I want to be well."
- "I don't want to fail" to "I want to succeed."
- "I don't want financial insecurity" to "I want to build a profitable business."

Knowing what you do not want defines what you do want. However, what you truly desire must be as *clear* and as *specific* as possible. (See "Rapid Business Growth for Financial Freedom" by Arlene Krantz on page 85.)

Secret Three: Focus and Align

Now that you know what you want, your focus must be on it, not on the absence of it. Esther and Jerry Hicks state in their book, *Ask and It is Given,* published by Hay House in 2004, "Even though a clear desire has emanated from you as a result of the contrast you have considered, you often, rather than giving your attention purely to the desire itself, focus back on the contrasting situation."

An example might be that you want to make a six-figure income next year. This idea excites you, yet every time you pay a bill, you complain that you do not have enough money and cannot afford the things you want. You wonder how you are ever going to make six figures. As long as you give your attention to what you *do not* want, what you *do* want cannot come to you.

Avoid getting stuck in the *how*—"*How* is this going to happen," "*How* is this possible?"

Figuring out *how* is not your job. The Universe responds to your asking and can provide possibilities and opportunities you cannot even dream about. Tell a different story about your financial situation and focus on what is coming. This aligns you with what you want.

Expect it to happen! It may seem difficult to make the distinction between actually thinking about your six-figure income and "beating the drum" of "I never have enough money." The next secret shows you how to know when you are really creating what you want.

Secret Four: Tune in to Your Own GPS System

Just like the GPS system in your car tells you if you are on the right track to where you want to go, you have your own guidance system— your emotions.

If you are feeling good, you are *allowing* what you want to come to you. Negative emotions are your indicator that you have introduced a vibration of what you "don't want" and are no longer in the state of allowing. This does not mean you should suppress your emotions— emotions can give you a key to an action step. Anger can sometimes mean, "My boundaries have been violated, and I need to speak up."

Imagine you repeatedly use the affirmation, "I am rich" and focus on being rich. When you look in your wallet, you realize you are broke and cannot even afford lunch. This creates doubt, discouragement and fear—certainly not a vibrational match to wealth! However, if you focus on the affirmation, "I am in the process of becoming rich," your emotion changes to hope and positive expectation.

Stay in the "feel-good feeling place" as much as possible! Many of us are careful about how we dress and how we look. However, we are sloppy about the way we think and feel. This affects our level of success since our thoughts and feelings create our life.

Secret Five: Change Limiting Beliefs at the Cellular Level

This is an excerpt of a process I developed to change singular beliefs at the cellular level. You can use it with some limiting beliefs you may have that could be sabotaging the secrets to success I've shared.

Read the entire process before beginning.

1. Sit comfortably and place your hand on your heart. As you do so, put your attention on your heart.

2. Take a deep breath and as you exhale, center your breath into your heart. Inhale and exhale several times as you breathe into your heart, feeling relaxed.

3. Say the following statement, "These teachings are energetically downloaded and saved into every cell of my body."

4. Read the statements below, one at a time. At the end of each statement say, "Yes!" aloud or silently, then take a deep breath into your heart and feel the energy flow throughout your body.

- I would like to know that I am *good enough.*

- I would like to know what it feels like to be good enough.

- I would like to know the highest definition and perspective on money.

- I would like to know that money is just an exchange.

- I would like to know it is okay for me to have more money than I need.

- I would like to know how to succeed without struggle, what it feels like and that it is possible.

- I would like to know how to focus on what I want rather than what I fear from the highest perspective.

- I would like to recognize when I am *allowing* success, how to allow success and that I am *worthy* of success.

- I want to know that it is safe for me to *feel good* and safe for others for me to feel good.

- I want to know when to take *action,* how to recognize the right action for me and how to take action with grace and ease.

- I want to know that, when I listen to my inner voice, the Universe supports me.

Remember to say "Yes!" at the end of *each* statement. By saying yes, you become a co-creator in these belief changes, and you give them more power and depth. You program your beliefs to change at the subconscious level by accessing your cell's own divine intelligence.

When you finish this process, notice what is different in the coming week—about how you view success and the steps I have shared. What is different in other areas of your life? The subconscious often has a benefit in *not* changing specific beliefs around success. If you feel blocked, put your hand on your heart or abdomen and imagine yourself being wildly successful. What *emotion* comes up? As you have seen, the subconscious may experience stress in areas where the conscious mind sees benefits, so explore your feelings.

Secret Six: Take Action

Renewed interest in the age-old concept of the *Law of Attraction* was catapulted into mainstream, popular culture by the book *The Secret* by Rhonda Byrnes, published by Simon and Schuster in 2006. These processes simply state that what you think about, you bring about. If you keep thinking about debt, failure and ill health, you get more of them.

Despite its success, people were disappointed in their ability to bring about what they wanted by just using the principles in the book. One big principle that was missing was action. As you know, the word "action" is in the *Law of Attraction.*

You know you need to take action. What kind of action is the right one to take? For some people, the Universe or God provides guidance if you ask. By saying, "Show me" and staying aware of signals, you will discover your next step.

If you were going to go for a walk in the dark, you would take a flashlight. If you shine it way out in front of you, you cannot see where you are going. If you shine it down by your feet, you can take one step at a time until you reach your destination. You can really never go wrong because if you do not like where your steps are taking you, you can always choose another path.

These six secrets to super success are really "the secrets" behind *The Secret*. By understanding the secrets and applying the information and processes, you can identify and release limiting beliefs that block you from succeeding as an entrepreneur. By taking time to work through the secrets, you will gain the self-confidence and self-empowerment you need to become a woman entrepreneur extraordinaire!

Special *Woman Entrepreneur Extraordinaire* Offer

Are subconscious beliefs keeping you from reaching your entrepreneurial dream? Receive a free, twenty-minute phone consultation in which I will utilize my belief change process to identify and change beliefs at the cellular level in one area. Unlock subconscious blocks and harness your power of success! Mention offer WESecrets.

BEVERLY LENZ, RN, MS

Discover your power to make changes

(760) 345-0347
beverly@beliefchangesystems.com
www.beliefchangesystems.com

Since 2003, Beverly Lenz has been developing and using belief change techniques that led her to formulate Belief Change Systems™. Utilizing her own unique, cutting-edge methods, she has become a transformational expert helping others master their mindset at a cellular level quickly and easily, revealing their potential in business and life. Beverly teaches her life-changing methods through seminars and workshops and is a licensed provider by the state of California for continuing education credits for medical professionals.

With a background in psychology, a bachelor of science degree in nursing and a master of science in management, Beverly has extensive counseling experience and training in crisis intervention, team building, group empowerment and relationships. Her unparalleled process helps release post-traumatic stress disorder effortlessly. She has helped businesses and individuals become more productive, prosperous and empowered, as well as happier and healthier. Her acclaimed classes, workshops and newsletters have made her a sought-after speaker and mentor for individuals, groups and companies.

Beverly is at the forefront of belief change at the cellular level. This is the true mind-body connection, and it is becoming the cornerstone for the science of the millennium.

The Ten Commandments of Small Business Success

How You Can Avoid the Ten Common Legal Mistakes Entrepreneurs Make

By Nancy Lewellen, ESQ, JD, MBA

*M*any entrepreneurs believe they do not need or cannot afford an attorney's services. If you believe this, it can lead you into trouble! You might:

- Fail to set up and maintain the correct business entity.

- Not be able to knowledgably review contracts and leases.

- Not understand the full extent of your financial commitments.

- Make other mistakes you could easily avoid with legal advice from a business or real estate attorney.

Why take chances? This chapter describes ten common mistakes entrepreneurs make and tells you how to avoid or correct them. Being willing to spend a little money up front can often save you a lot of money and stress later on. I call these my *Ten Commandments of Small Business Success.*

Commandment One:
Thou Shalt Choose the Correct Entity for Your Business Type

Today, you can choose among the following business entity types:

- Sole proprietorship: one-owner business

- S corporation: one or more owners, no double taxation

- C corporation: one or more owners, double taxation possible

- Close corporation: 35 or fewer owners

- PC or Professional Corporation: typically for legal, accounting or medical specialties

- LLC or Limited Liability Company: one or more owners, a hybrid between partnership and corporation

- GP or General Partnership: two or more owners, equal liabilities

- LP or Limited Partnership: two or more owners with varying liabilities

- LLP or Limited Liability Partnership: two or more owners with varying liabilities

- LLLP or Limited Liability Limited Partnership: two or more owners with varying liabilities

Throughout this chapter, I will use the word "Company" or "Companies," with a capital "C" to denote Corporations, PCs, LLCs, LPs, LLPs and LLLPs, but not sole proprietorships or general partnerships.

Choosing the right business entity has many benefits and can protect your personal assets from being attached if your business is sued and you lose. Each Company type has specific ongoing requirements, ranging from simple to complex. The following is a partial list of things to consider when selecting the right business entity. Confer with your tax professional before choosing your entity, since each has different tax consequences.

Here are some things to consider:

Cost of setting up and maintaining the entity. A sole proprietorship is the simplest and least costly entity. The other entities are more expensive to set up and maintain, and typically require lawyers or paralegals to draft the operating agreement and file the necessary governmental paperwork. They usually take longer to receive back governmentally-approved documents. C corporations may have *double* taxation—net profits are taxed, as are the salary and dividends of any Company officers. However, S corporations do not have double taxation.

Personal assets at risk. If you do not have significant personal assets, you may not need to incur the expense and time to set up and maintain one of the more complex entities. If someone successfully sues your business, the plaintiffs likely will get little or nothing. However, if a judgment is levied against your business, and you draw compensation as a Company employee, or you later work for someone else, your wages could be garnished for years to come to satisfy the judgment.

If you are a sole proprietor who is not a Company and someone sues you, they are essentially suing you, the person, not your business. If they win and you go to work for someone else, your wages could be garnished to satisfy the personal judgment.

Time and expense involved observing corporate or LLC formalities. Corporate or LLC formalities include holding and documenting shareholder meetings, not commingling business and personal assets and drafting corporate or LLC resolutions among other things. Observing corporate or LLC formalities takes time and creates additional expenses that a sole proprietorship does not have. See Commandment Two. On the other hand, the sole proprietor has no formalities to observe.

Tax consequences. If you are a Company, you may need to file separate tax returns. If you are a sole proprietor or GP, you report income and expenses on your personal tax return. Companies get tax deductions for employee benefits and may depreciate expensive assets.

Certain professions cannot be LLCs. In some states, certain professions, like law, medicine, accounting, architecture, chiropractic or veterinary, cannot be LLCs. Each may only be a sole proprietor, PC, LP, LLP or LLLP.

Health care benefits. If your Company has two or more owners/employees, the Company qualifies for guaranteed-issue group benefits. Group benefits often have lower out-of-pocket dollar risk exposure. Generally, a sole proprietor is not eligible for group insurance.

Commandment Two:
Thou Shalt Observe Corporate Formalities

Many entrepreneurs establish Companies thinking that they have permanent personal liability protection. *This is incorrect.*

Unlike sole proprietors, Companies are viewed as legal persons separate from their owners. This legal view protects your personal assets from outsiders suing the Company. *However, this protection is not absolute.* An outsider suing a Company may "pierce the corporate veil" and reach your personal assets. To avoid this, Company owners must *continually* observe *corporate formalities* that show the Company is separate from them as individuals. What are these corporate or LLC formalities? The list is long and usually includes the items listed on the following page.

- Keeping personal and Company assets separate by establishing a Company bank account, purchasing Company assets with Company cash and purchasing personal assets with personal funds.

- Drafting, signing and dating Company resolutions for important decisions affecting the Company.

- Having written Company policies and employee handbooks.

- Having owners and officers vote on important matters.

- Holding and documenting frequent Company meetings to review important issues.

- Keeping current any necessary Company licenses.

- Withholding taxes from officers' and employees' wages.

Commandment Three:
Thou Shalt Not Comingle Company and Personal Assets

As you have read, it is imperative to keep Company and personal assets separate. What are some tips to accomplish this?

- Write and sign Company resolutions at the time of meetings that confirm your previous actions to purchase large Company assets, such as vehicles or office equipment.

- Repay yourself from Company profits with Company checks for personal money spent on Company purchases.

- Have Company owners purchase stock or membership shares to raise cash for the Company. If you have purchased a large item, such as equipment or vehicles, have the Company issue a promissory note to pay you back with interest. Put the title of the vehicle in the Company name, and name yourself as the lender on the owner-ship certificate.

Commandment Four:
Thou Shalt Have an Attorney Review Your Lease

You would not operate on yourself, fill your own teeth or prepare complicated tax returns because you are not qualified to do so. Yet, many entrepreneurs sign complicated leases for premises, often for long periods, without really understanding their commitment. Here are some common problems to be aware of:

- Realize you may be taking on tens of thousands of dollars in liabilities over lease payments because of the "fine print" in the lease.

- How you sign a lease determines who is liable for the rent in the event the Company goes out of business.

- Document in writing any damage caused by a previous tenant. Make it part of the lease and have the landlord sign it, so you are not liable for these same damages when you leave the premises.

Commandment Five:
Thou Shalt Plan for Management Succession

Owners of small businesses often fail to plan for management succession. Management succession plans detail who becomes the Company owner when the original owner is no longer there, due to death, disability, illness or other reasons. If you are a business co-owner, you could end up working with your co-owner's spouse if you live in a community property state and your co-owner dies. If your co-owner becomes disabled, what happens to his or her share of the business? Can you afford to replace your partner or buy out his or her share? Some inexpensive steps can prevent these events from closing your doors. A sole proprietor can create this agreement with a trusted employee, relative or other person so his/her surviving spouse gets money from the sale of the business.

- Obtaining Company key-person life insurance on the co-owners provides needed cash or pays business expenses, so the surviving spouse does not have to do so.

- Obtaining Company disability insurance on co-owners helps pay for a disabled co-owner's share of rent and other expenses. A second disability policy with the co-owner's spouse as beneficiary can pay for personal and medical expenses during disability periods.

- Creating a "buy-sell agreement" when a business is new details how the co-owners' shares can be bought out, how their value will be calculated and what happens to their shares in the event of death, disability or leaving the business. The agreement allows for the business' survival after one or more original co-owners is gone. The buy-sell agreement should have a non-compete clause, so an angry, departing co-owner does not set up shop across the street and become your main competitor. Many business attorneys can provide these documents.

- Having spouses sign the buy-sell agreement means the spouses agree not to take ownership of the Company if their spouse leaves, dies or becomes disabled. In addition, they will not put their spouse's ownership in any trust or will they may make later.

Commandment Six:
Thou Shalt Not Review and Draft Your Own Contracts

Many entrepreneurs copy contract provisions from the Internet, friends' businesses and other places. I often see these clients when:

- The customer does not pay his or her bill.

- The client uses a contract phrase in a way that was unintended.

- The entrepreneur tries to enforce the contract and discovers there are conflicting clauses that cancel out each other.

- Important contract issues are omitted.

Often, *an attorney cannot undo* the damage done by a poorly drafted, signed contract or lease. You may end up paying a lot more in legal fees than you would have paid to have a good contract or a lease drafted, reviewed or negotiated. Spending some money up front can save you a lot of money and headache later and prevent parties from settling disputes through costly litigation, mediation or arbitration.

Commandment Seven:
Thou Shalt Not Operate Your Business without a License

I frequently see people who fail to keep a calendar showing when professional or business licenses expire or who send in renewal fees late. Many professions, such as law, medicine, certified public accounting and real estate brokerage, require a certain number of hours of continuing education to keep a license in good standing. Some prohibit operating with an expired license.

Many entrepreneurs fail to pay for general business licenses required by the government in order to keep operating at their current location. This can result in costly interest and penalties. In some states, California for example, mortgage brokers and general contractors cannot be paid unless they have a current license. Mark your calendar with important license expiration dates, so this does not happen to you!

Some businesses, such as a traveling food truck, child day-care facilities in a residential neighborhood or pet day-care centers may require a variance from the zoning in the area in which their business is located before they can obtain a license. Yet many of these owners are unaware when they sign a lease that they may not be able to open their doors until this variance is approved by the local government. Check the zoning before you sign a lease to ascertain whether zoning in the area where you want to do business will allow you to do so.

Commandment Eight:
Thou Shalt Not Confuse Business with Personal Liability

One of the easiest ways you can unknowingly obligate yourself personally is by incorrectly signing leases and other contracts. Make sure you sign the Company name and then your title as follows:

Correct:

Doggone Doggie, Inc.

Dewey, Cheatham & Howe, LLP

By: _____
Sam Schnauzer, President

By: _____
Susie Cheatham, General Partner

Incorrect:

_____
Sam Schnauzer

_____
Doggone Doggie, Inc.

Despite your best attempts to keep business and personal liabilities separate, some vendors or landlords may ask for a personal guarantee if you are a new entrepreneur. By signing a personal guarantee, you will owe money up to the dollar limit on the guarantee for the Company's debts if the Company is unable to pay.

What can a new entrepreneur do? You may be able to negotiate the amount on the personal guarantee down to a fixed-dollar amount that is smaller than the amount of the contract or lease. In my experience, when parties negotiate, they usually get some portion of what they ask for.

If you have a personal vehicle you need to operate in your business, you might consider selling the vehicle to the Company and getting insurance in the Company's name. If later you have an accident while on Company business, the Company will likely be liable for damages.

Be careful who you let use the vehicle. An attorney I know collected a multi-million dollar judgment for his client, a young boy who was run over by a corporate worker who was driving under the influence. The attorney proved the corporation owned the truck and routinely allowed its employees to personally use it after hours as part of their employee benefits. The Company was thus liable for the boy's medical expenses and pain-and-suffering settlement.

If you are a sole proprietor who is not a Company and injure someone while driving for your business, you are personally liable. There is no corporate protection. A sole proprietor does not get this protection.

Commandment Nine:
Thou Shalt Get Permission to Use Famous Names in Your Company Name

If you wish to use a famous name in your business name or use a unique logo, have an attorney do an inexpensive, simple search of trademark, service mark or copyright. After the search, you may be able to use a protected name or logo by signing a licensing or royalty agreement with the possessor of the mark. If the name is not being used, you can get your own copyright, trademark or service mark, which will prevent others from stealing it. This can save you the pain and expense of a lawsuit down the road, which can shut down your business.

Commandment Ten:
Thou Shalt Safeguard Business Finances

Co-owners sometimes spend money without conferring with one another. Occasionally, I find a client's co-owner has embezzled money or obligated the Company in some way my client did not foresee or know about. How can you avoid this?

- Incorporate into your operating agreement or bylaws a maximum dollar amount that one person can authorize on his or her own signature.

- Require multiple signatures on Company checking accounts or contracts for expenditures in excess of a specified dollar amount and print the dollar amount above the Company signature line.

- Insist on monthly meetings to go over Company finances.

- Depending on your Company ownership and officer status, you may be able to vote the offending party out of the Company.

- If neither you nor your co-owners are good at finances, employ the services of a bookkeeper, CPA or Enrolled Agent.

Follow My Ten Commandments to Entrepreneurial Success

As an entrepreneur, you are an expert in your field. By allowing other experts, such as attorneys and accountants to help you, you often can save time, money and stress associated with operating your Company. There is an old expression, "He who acts as his own attorney has a fool for a client."

By using other experts, you may avoid costly mistakes that can put you out of business! Using an attorney need not be expensive nor something to dread. They can be a silent partner in your business, helping you grow and thrive.

Special *Woman Entrepreneur Extraordinaire* Offer

Sign up on my mailing list and receive *free* newsletters with legal and marketing tips. Get a free e-book on the costs and benefits of setting up LLCs, Corporations or LLPs, comparing the pros and cons of each, in a simple-to-read format. A $25.00 value—*free*. Visit www.palladianlawgroup.com to sign up.

NANCY LEWELLEN, ESQ, JD, MBA
Attorney at Law

(415) 399-0993
nyl@palladianlawgroup.com
www.palladianlawgroup.com

Nancy Lewellen is a California-licensed attorney, real estate broker and managing partner of Palladian Law Group™. Her practice emphasizes business, real estate and wills/trust law. She helps individuals, small businesses and non-profits set up and maintain corporations, LLCs, LLPs, and LLLPs; drafts, negotiates and reviews contracts and leases; advises on landlord/tenant, boundary, and short sale and foreclosure issues; and mediates, arbitrates or litigates when necessary.

Her business background allows Nancy to focus on her clients' businesses in addition to legal issues. She is a trained mediator with certificates in international and public interest law from Santa Clara University School of Law and a masters of business administration in finance and international business. Before law school, Nancy was an international, corporate and consumer bank lender and had her own commercial and residential mortgage brokerage businesses. Nancy speaks Spanish.

Nancy is an ambassador with Business Network International (BNI)®, past-president and current membership chair of her BNI chapter, member of Queen's Bench, the City Club and Golden Gate Business Association. She is a frequent public speaker. Nancy has two daughters, Kim and Heather, and a "grand dog," Osiris.

Using Courage to Create Your Legacy

Discover Paths to your Personal
Success and Ideal Life

By Sylvia Guinan, MBA

*D*o you have the feeling there is something greater out there waiting for you, some level of success that is larger and more meaningful? Good! That is your legacy calling you. Success is not some elusive standard only meant for others. It is meant for everyone, especially *you*. Yes, there are secrets to success. One of its best-kept secrets is how you define it for your own life. That's right! All this time you may have been keeping the secret of success from yourself.

It is time to reveal what your success looks like and what your life can become.

Your success is a deeply personal decision. No one can decide or define what success means for you. You will not find it written in a magazine, or on a reality show or by following someone else's formula. It is *your* success. You must embrace what success means for you and be consistently intentional in reaching your goals.

For most, true success will be achieved when all aspects of their life are working together in a smooth synergy, all focused on the same meaningful financial and personal goals. Of course, something this powerful does not just fall into place. Like everything else with long-lasting, even eternal, purpose, you must invest the time and energy on yourself and work at it every day.

For instance, by visualizing, defining and implementing an invest-ment plan to support your personal goals you are building a foundation for what needs to occur within your business to achieve the most personal dreams for your life. This is why your plan of success must begin with your own set of goals. In other words, decide where you specifically want to go in all aspects of your life by determining how they all work together. When you do, you will begin to have a good, grounded sense of purpose.

As a dynamic woman who is empowered to create new opportunities through entrepreneurial and personal development, it is time to put doubt aside and move forward. You should start to experience significant change in your life the moment you begin to look at yourself as a *courageous entrepreneur.* The tools in this chapter help you to journey inward and genuinely explore what matters most both professionally and personally. This provides a template to gather detailed information and implement a thorough investment plan, one designed to show you the way to your financial destination. By putting it into a measurable, manageable plan, you should be able to clearly see how you are tracking in achieving both your business and personal financial goals.

The Three C's

Once you articulate and make a specific plan to reach your customized, ideal lifestyle, the time will come to work with your financial advisor to put all of this information into a well-defined personal investment plan. The ideal plan, the one you deserve, is developed through clarity, consolidation and a sense of control.

Clarity

"The future belongs to those
who believe in the beauty of their dreams."
—Eleanor Roosevelt, American,
former first lady of the United States

Use visualization and become clear about what your ideal life will look like down to the smallest detail. Take uninterrupted time for yourself to visualize and define your life in the years to come. The more clearly you can see it, the more likely you may achieve it.

By defining your *ideal* versus your merely *acceptable* goals, you create side roads and alternate routes to take you on the journey to your ultimate destination. In life, there isn't just one clear cut route to take. There are many options. *You* set the course based on how and what is most important to *you* at the time. For example, as a mother of three young children whom I adore, I realize every day has a certain element of unpredictability. Recently, while stopped at a railroad crossing, I saw a sign that read, *Expect a Train!* That spoke volumes to me. In order to find balance, I accept the fact that I must expect the unexpected.

As women, mothers, and professionals, who love our families and our careers (Yes, it is okay to admit we find fulfillment in both!), we must remain resolute in achieving balance through consistent and intentional focus on our ultimate destination.

This means clearly defining what your *ideal* future goals are from what your acceptable goals are. *Ideal goals* consist of your hopes and dreams *without limitations. Acceptable goals* are those you are willing to compromise in order to reach your ultimate goals. Once you have explored and articulated them, share them with your financial advisor, so that together, you can use them as a benchmark in your life plan. Below are some guidelines to help get you started.

Getting Started

Use your dream board as a financial tool. A dream board is a fun, ongoing process. It is a deeply personal, visual representation of your goals. Start by finding photos representing your dreams-come-true and attach them to poster board. Do not limit yourself. Remember, no one else has to see this. You get to decide your dreams, so only you will decide what to put on your dream board. Then, translate what you see to a written list of goals. You will share this list with your financial advisor.

Keep a financial journal. The written word is extremely powerful in helping turn your goals and dreams into the life you desire. It will take some discipline, so keep a journal and jot down your thoughts as they come to mind. If you often wake up with your mind racing over something you want, like a new car, a vacation, a new home or your retirement, write it down immediately. Putting things in writing is one of the best ways to clarify what is on your mind. Invest the time and start the habit today. It will help to remove the distraction of *thought clutter* while creating momentum for success.

Define major life goals. Do not wait one minute. Every moment you delay is one more lost opportunity. Once you have defined your major life goals, separate them into steps that describe what needs to happen in the next three years, one year, three months, and *tomorrow* to get you on course.

Prioritize your goals. Remember, *ideal goals* consist of your hopes and dreams *without limitations*. *Acceptable goals* are those you are willing to compromise in order to reach your ultimate goals.

Establish a list of your goals in the order of importance to you. Consider goals that are firm—your *musts*—and the ones on which you are willing to compromise—your *mights*. For example, you may say you would like to work until age 62 and create an ongoing, lifetime annual income of $175,000. When your advisor creates your plan, she may come back and tell you that there is only a 35 percent chance of reaching that goal. You may then decide that working a few more years to age 64 and spending $150,000 annually for all your expenses is acceptable. By working a little longer and spending a little less, you may increase the chance of success by up to 90 percent. (This information is hypothetical and is provided for informational purposes only. Investors should make their own decisions based on their specific investment objectives and financial circumstances.)

Remember, *you always have choices.* You may decide to work harder and earn more over the next ten years, so you are more likely to achieve your original goals, or you may decide the alternate option is acceptable.

Consolidation

Gather information on all the financial items you have acquired thus far. These include savings, investment accounts, 401k accounts, IRAs and insurance. Also, gather information on the *liability side* of your balance sheet, such as credit card debt, car loans, student loans, mortgage and any home equity lines of credit. Work with your financial advisor to consolidate all the information into your plan.

Do not forget the importance of your personal goals. These should include items like how long you want to work, how much income you will need annually, the lifestyle you would like to lead and where you would like to spend your time. Remember to include special purchases you want to make, such as travel, family and philanthropic goals and so on. This complete scenario helps build your legacy.

The plans I prepare for my clients include examples in order to illustrate side-by-side how certain goals can affect the plan. Your investment plan is designed to help show you the likelihood of success based on the different goals versus your financial assets.

Five essential pillars of wealth management. Begin by gathering as much detail as you can on each of these five areas of your financial life. Be certain to have your financial advisor include this information in your overall investment plan:

1. Financial information. Gather statements on your investments, savings, IRAs, Roth IRAs, 401ks and other investments

2. Retirement planning. Understand your retirement goals and what you need to do to help achieve them. Make sure your business is maximizing all the retirement saving options available to you and your employees.

3. Estate information. Update your wills, trusts, power of attorney, health care proxies, insurance policy beneficiaries and IRA beneficiaries. Make sure all this is current. If you have a business partner, it is essential their information also be current.

4. Liability information. Include business loans, personal loans, credit cards, mortgages and home equity lines of credit.

5. Family planning. If you have children or grandchildren, you may want to explore college saving options, living expenses and the legacy you want to leave. Many of my clients are also planning to help and care for their parents, which may include home care, extended living facilities and health insurance.

In the course of my role as a financial advisor, I have seen enormous, life-altering changes in the outlooks and priorities of my clients. These are mostly caused by drastic changes in the economy and financial markets. For instance, 12 years ago, the most common goal I saw was the desire to leave a legacy for their children. Today, most of my clients are concerned with leading a comfortable retirement and being able to take care of their finances while maintaining their lifestyle well into their 90s. Their goals have changed from leaving a legacy to avoiding becoming a burden on their children. If there is anything left over for a legacy, they consider that a plus.

Work with your financial advisor to put all of your information into one cohesive investment plan. This is the foundation for all the work you will do with your advisor. The investment plan dictates how your assets will be managed in accordance with what you need to achieve. To track your individual progress and help empower your destiny, you may want to have your financial advisor give you an easily understood graph in your monthly financial statement. This gives you a visual measure of your ongoing mission to reach your goals.

Control

"The best way to predict the future is to create it."
—Author unknown

In my office, I have a weathered wooden plaque with the quote above. I make it a point to read and reflect on it daily. For my clients and me, it is a very powerful message because it reminds us that we are in control. A good friend of mine has a saying: "Ninety percent of your success and good fortune is created by the person you see in the mirror every day. Ten percent comes from luck and good timing."

Money is not what motivates individuals. It is what the money can do for you. Once you have a clear understanding of what you want to achieve, your information consolidated into a plan, and a sense of how you are moving toward your goals, you should be empowered with a greater sense of control for your future. You will also understand what compromises and sacrifices need to be made and decide what matters to you the most. All of this will help empower you with self-determination and fulfillment. Once you know how well you are tracking, you can adjust your goals and priorities to help you achieve what matters most to you. Again, the most empowering dynamic of this process is the understanding of how much control you gain for your future.

Next Steps

Take one step at a time. Set precise goals, with dates, times and amounts, so you can take the appropriate steps to measure the results. Remember this simple rule: You cannot manage your success if you cannot measure it. It will help your process if you know where you are supposed to be by certain dates.

Balance personal and business goals. You have a drive to bring meaning to your own life and those of the people around you. Think of balance as a way of adding joy, productivity and positive energy to each moment.

Dream big. Great aspirations consist of many small steps, so focus on taking steps daily to get you closer to your dream. This will help give you a sense of purpose as well as keep you motivated. You will be amazed at how far you can go by taking just a few steps every day.

Keep your ideal and acceptable goals current. I recommend you monitor your goals quarterly at the very least. It is amazing how much things can change in just 90 days.

Monitor the plan on an ongoing basis with your advisor. Depending on the complexity of your situation, schedule semi-annual or annual reviews. If you experience significant changes in the interim, immediately reach out to your financial advisor, so they can update your plan.

Acknowledge your accomplishments. Keep your eye on the ultimate goal and make sure you take time along the way to recognize all that you have done so far. Give yourself credit. You are doing something very important—something not all people do.

Make a commitment to stay focused on your goals. Strive to reach your goals with enthusiasm and a high regard for yourself. Every journey begins with a single step, and in many ways, this sets the tone for the entire trip. Your progress will be rewarding when you make each step you take count.

Focus on the best outcome. By defining what you want to achieve and taking action, you put yourself on the path to success. Do not allow fear or limitations to get in the way. This means no more negative *what-ifs*. Focus on thinking about what the best possible outcome looks like.

Your mission statement is not set in stone. Take time annually to review your mission statement and adjust your business and personal goals. If your priorities change, so can your mission statement. It is your life. *You* make the rules.

Try on your future. At least once every day, imagine what it feels like to be living your ideal life. Then spend time daily taking steps to get you there.

This Is Your Moment

Right now, you are standing at a crossroads. What you do next may determine the quality of your life for decades to come. It may determine your relationships, your business, your family and your legacy. Yes, this is perhaps the most personal decision you will ever make. You can start right now.

Take a few minutes and write down three things you will do in the next 48 hours to uncover your dreams and make them come true: start your dream board, schedule an appointment with your financial advisor, put aside the time you need to get a clear vision for how you want your life to be and so on. Do *whatever* it takes to start you on your journey. The decision is *yours*.

SYLVIA GUINAN, MBA
Financial Advisor
Associate Vice President – Investments
Wells Fargo Advisors, LLC

(860) 767-2681
sylvia.guinan@wfadvisors.com
www.sylviaguinan.wfadv.com

Sylvia Guinan is an Associate Vice President—Investments at Wells Fargo Advisors in Essex, Connecticut. She focuses her practice on working with women going through divorce, career transitions and loss of a spouse. Through planning, investment strategies and on-going education, Sylvia helps identify and prioritize her client's goals and empowers them by increasing their knowledge and confidence in making financial decisions. She also collaborates with her client's other professional advisors to work as a team to help meet the client's goals.

Sylvia has appeared on the *Better Connecticut Show* and *Eyewitness News, Channel 3* on topics relating to women and investing. She has also been on the *Mary Jones Radio Show* on *WDRC* covering topics on planning for women.

Sylvia has a master of business administration from St. John's University. She is the chair of the board for the Eastern Connecticut division of the American Heart Association®. She is also on the board of the Westbrook Economic Development Committee. Sylvia is a non-attorney member of the *Connecticut Bar Association.*

Rapid Business Growth for Financial Freedom

By Arlene Krantz, CHt, MD (TM)

*A*re there times when you feel so overwhelmed in your business that it is hard to get up in the morning and start your day? Do you sometimes dread going to your office because you know your business is nowhere near what you wanted when you first started?

If you are like many of my clients, I bet you are nodding your head, "Yes." Well, there is hope. What you need is a business coach who mentors and guides you to financial freedom doing what you love—and does it fast! In this chapter, I will work with you to give you a game plan, so you *break through your money issues to financial freedom in 90 days or less* and finally enjoy the success you have always wanted.

> *"You are surrounded by simple, obvious solutions that can dramatically increase your income, power, influence and success. The problem is, you just don't see them."*
> —Jay Abraham, American marketing consultant

Quiet Your Inner Critic around Money and Success

You know that little voice from your subconscious that whispers, "You can't." Don't you just want to say, "Shut the heck up"?

Well, you can.

The first thing you want to work on is clearing your mind to move onto building your business and making money with speed. (See "Master the Secrets for Entrepreneurial Success" by Beverly Lenz on page 49 for more information on clearing.)

You can do many exercises when you hear that voice, and they work. Some of the ones that you could use are:

Emotional freedom techniques® (EFT). When you use EFT, also known as *tapping,* you *tap* along your meridians to clear out negative messages and feelings you want to get rid of when they occur. Negative emotions disturb the body's energy system, so tapping releases these emotions and brings harmony back into your body. As you tap, you take a series of thoughts from negative to positive. Many websites explain how to tap, and you can tap along with the instructors. Check this out to see how it works. Having a business coach who does tapping with you while you are working together is a big plus. It certainly cleared up many negative thoughts for me when I was working with my business coach.

Deep breathing. Right now, stop reading and take three, deep breaths—really deep and slow. Are you surprised how much calmer you feel? When you work out with a trainer, he or she often tells you to stop holding your breath and breathe while you are doing an exercise. This also works when you are working hard and become anxious. Your body needs to let go of this stress and anxiety, and deep breathing is an instant fix for this. Remember to take three deep, slow breaths whenever you need them as slow breathing produces calmness, and your body will thank you.

Self-hypnosis. This is a wonderful way to loosen up and get rid of stress. If you want to see how this works, go to this website—www. wikihow.com/Perform-Self-Hypnosis, which will explain how you do it. When I work with my clients, I make a custom CD for them to achieve a deep state of relaxation that helps them clear their minds and reinvigorate their business thoughts. Very important: *Do not do this while driving.* You can do-it-yourself with these tips:

• Find a quiet place with no interruption, no phones, no computer—a place you can be alone for at least one-half hour.

• Uncross your hands and feet.

• Close your eyes and take five, deeps breaths inhaling through your nose.

• With every exhale, say the word, "relax."

• You will notice your breathing slowing down as you relax more and more.

• Feel your muscles relaxing as you continue to breathe slowly and deeply.

• Imagine or visualize you are at the top of a staircase with twenty stairs. Put your left foot out to go down the first stair and hold on to the railing.

• With each step down, you will go deeper and deeper into a relaxed state.

• At the bottom of the stairs is a door. When you open that door, you will be in a place that is special to you. Maybe it is the beach, or maybe it is the forest. It does not matter as long as it is special for you.

• Let your senses take over. Taste, smell, feel everything. Your body will appreciate this time of peace and quiet.

• Believe in yourself while you are in this relaxed state.

- When you are ready to leave this peaceful place, climb the stairs.

- When you reach the top, you say, "wide awake" a few times until you feel alert and wide awake.

(See also "Break Free to Six Figures" by Georgina Sweeney on page 209 for more information on how to overcome negative imprints.)

How Much Do You Want?

Your subconscious only knows what it knows. Get a financial image of how much money you want to make by creating a mental picture. See the money in your bank account. Watch yourself buying a new car or a new house. Take your friends out to a fabulous dinner. Give money to your favorite charity.

How does it feel to be stress-free around money? Feel the emotion of having abundance in your life. Get very clear on what you really want, so you can get your game plan in motion and have this money coming in quickly.

"Your subconscious is like millions of workers in a corporation and they are just waiting for instructions from the CEO—your conscious mind."
—Michael Stevenson,
American master NLP practitioner and teacher

What Path Are You Taking?

This is one loaded question! When you go into business, you have one thought in mind. Somewhere along the way, however, things change. Maybe you want to take another path in your business that you had not thought of before, or you like where you are going and need help to stay on this path.

I want you to love your business with passion, so really think of *what you really want to do*. This applies to all aspects of your life and work.

Do not use the computer for this exercise. Take a paper and pencil and write out your answers. Let them come from the subconscious. Just sit in a quiet place, undisturbed. Getting this out of your subconscious creates clarity and freedom to start thinking creatively.

Some questions you might want to ask yourself are:

• What would you like to learn?

Leslie is a hot air balloon pilot and loves what she does. She also loves working on her computer and found that she was a fast learner. We explored her options, and she is now pursuing her goal as an online business manager. Leslie is also working with me on our new website called "Amazing Women in Action," and we're loving it. So much to learn!

• What skills do you want to develop?

Can you see yourself becoming the photographer you always wanted to be? Learning how to work your camera and taking the photographs for your business marketing and even more. Can you envision your tabletop book on sale at the bookstore! By getting the income you so deserve you have that choice to grab on to that dream of yours and snap away.

• Can you describe your perfect life?

The sun is shining down on you as you are sitting in your sarong by the beach in Costa Rica drinking a piña colada. This could be your reality if you believe you can make the money you deserve. Are you charging enough? Everything in life is possible if you make a money goal, have a solid plan and then just go for it.

- How much money do you want to make monthly and annually and how soon do you want to make this money?

  PJ is taking his business from the low five figures to six figures in just six months and now is setting his two-year goals for seven figures. He is growing very fast and is making the money he deserves because he is charging what he is worth.

- Whom do you want to be friends with?

  I would love to have Oprah on my friend list and be invited to a weekend at her estate in Montecito, California. It hasn't happened yet, and you never know what life has in store for you!

- Where do you want to live?

  We live in a global world and just think about walking the streets of Roma, stopping for a cappuccino at a café with your laptop while chatting over the Internet to a client in Brazil. Ah, love the Italians and the Internet. It's all possible if you believe you can make the income to allow yourself to make this change. Living in an apartment overlooking the Coliseum, wow, what a life and you can have it too.

  It's all in the planning.

What Are You Doing NOW to Get It?

Are you planning your everyday activities toward producing the amount of money you deserve on a monthly and yearly basis for a life full of abundance?

As a business coach, I want you to focus in on making money fast. Looking at what you do during the day is sometimes mind-blowing. Read each statement and answer "Yes" or "No."

- Are you devoting enough time and effort toward promoting your business? Close the computer, shut off the phone and focus on marketing your business. Clients are not going to knock at your door. You have to go out and get them.

- Do you advertise in the right places where your potential clients hang out? Find out what they read, where they go, what they like, where they shop. That is where you advertise and where you go.

- Are you targeting your market with what you think is the right message and find no one is responding? What words would your market use to describe themselves? Speak to them in *their* language.

- Do you know you have problems closing the sale and, therefore, lose clients? Script out your closing and get used to saying the words. Practice makes perfect.

- Do you feel you are not worth the money you ask for? Of course, you are worth it—and even more! You just have to ask for it.

- Are your customers complaining they are not getting the service they expected? Without customer service, you have no customers. Make sure you keep in touch with your clients and keep them happy. (See "Customer Service Cuts through Competition" by Sheri Brunnquell on page 131.)

- Are you finding it hard to believe in yourself? Re-read the section on EFT in this chapter, start tapping away those beliefs, know you are a fabulous person and deserve success.

Show Me the Money!

Now that you have taken care of the obstacles to having the money and success you want from your business, let's look at how much you charge for your services. Do you hear that little voice again? I'm sure you do! My clients have shared with me the following reasons why they cannot raise their prices. Do they sound familiar to you?

- I cannot ask for that much money!

- I am not worthy of asking for more.

- No one has any money.

- We are in an economic slowdown.

- Add your message here!

Go back to the beginning of this chapter and practice some of the strategies to quiet these voices. Now, follow these tips:

- **Think up.** Remember why you went into business in the first place and keep that vision in mind. Make yourself a vision board, put all the things you want in your life on that board and keep looking at it, so you do not lose that vision.

- **Charge more.** This is the fastest way to get money into your bank account and the easiest way to make more money. When you start asking for what you deserve, you will find very little resistance and will be pleasantly surprised. You will wish you had asked for more money sooner. If someone says they cannot afford you, tell them why they cannot afford *not to use* your services. If you believe it, so will your clients.

- **Always give your best.** When your client sees how hard you are working on their needs and how much you give of yourself, it makes them feel special and grateful for your involvement in their business. They will refer you, as well.

I Am in a Millionaire Mindset

You are now on your way to making changes to grow your business. No matter how many plans you make, how much research you do and how many teleseminars you listen to, if you do not take action, nothing happens. You need a million-dollar mindset for the road to financial freedom.

- **Create multiple streams of income.** When you give a talk, record it and sell the CD. Take that talk and make it into an ebook. There are so many ways to add value and products to what you do and increase your income. Isn't that what you want? (See "Information Products Equal Accelerated Cash Flow" by Michele Scism on page 155.)

- **Hire others to do what you don't want to do.** I am all for using others because I am not about to do what I cannot or really do not want to do. Bookkeeping, designing a website, writing ad copy, hiring a graphic artist—getting whatever and whomever you need to support you in your business and at home frees up your time to market your business. (See "Expand Your Business with an Effective Virtual Team" by Dortha Hise on page 165.)

- **Just do it.** If you are caught up in perfection, you will never get going. I cannot tell you how many times I have procrastinated because it was never going to be "good enough." I'm not making that mistake anymore and neither should you.

- **Open up your mind to new possibilities.** When an opportunity comes your way, take a good look and see if it fits into your goals and vision. Listen to what other people are doing and talk to them about leveraging your business with theirs. There are so many opportunities out there in the world. We just have to look and listen.

- **Be generous with others who need your help.** Volunteer at a soup kitchen, tutor schoolchildren to read, drive seniors to doctor's appointments. There are a myriad of places to volunteer. Just find the right one for you. And yes, write out that check, too.

Get a Good Business Coach

A business coach assists and guides you in developing your business. They help you be clear about your business goals, get past the mental blocks that stop you from achieving them, bring you back into focus and mentor you through all your fears and successes.

Most successful entrepreneurs use business coaches and mentors as they continue to grow their businesses. You are not in this alone, nor should you feel you need to do it by yourself. Reach out! Get the help you need. Ask your business friends if they can refer someone. Ask for references. Check out the website and see if what they say appeals to you. Ask them how they can help you in your particular situation. My favorite way to know if someone is the right person is to trust my intuition.

Here's to your success. Start now to rapidly grow your business!

Special *Woman Entrepreneur Extraordinaire* Offer

Discover how to build your business fast! Sign up for a free 30-minute "Money Breakthrough" strategy session with Arlene at arlene@ arlenekrantz.com.

ARLENE KRANTZ, CHt, MD (TM)

The Money Breakthrough Coach

*Double your business in
six months or less*

(310) 922-6822
arlene@arlenekrantz.com
www.arlenekrantz.com

Arlene Krantz began her business career in retail for two major specialty and department stores working her way from the sales floor to the buying office. She realized she did not want to work for anyone else and started her own business, taking it from zero to seven figures in three years. It was one heck of a ride and very rewarding.

Arlene then decided she wanted to explore her spirituality. She obtained certification as an advanced reiki training practitioner. She became a healer traveling the world and received a doctor of traditional medicine degree. Arlene then became a certified hypnotherapist, master NLP practitioner and master imagery practitioner. Yet, something was missing for Arlene.

For many years, Arlene instinctively helped others to grow their businesses because she loved doing it. She became a business coach as a natural segue back into the world of business. Arlene loves to work with clients who want fast results that put more money in their business. She lives in West Hollywood, California.

A Winning Business Plan Leads to Massive Success

By V. Lynn Hawkins

Whether you are starting from square one as a new business or you have been in business for years, having a good written business plan is the start of what can be a very lucrative journey to a destination called "massive success."

Most businesses can get to a destination called "success." However, wouldn't you rather go to "massive success?" Personally, I prefer "massive success,"—if that is the destination *you* want, then join me on this amazing journey!

There is an art to writing a winning business plan. Like any work of art, it requires a bit of time and effort to express the vision and then devise the strategy to make that vision a reality. What is really nice is that it can be simple to do. While writing a business plan may seem like a daunting task, it does not have to be an insurmountable challenge. In fact, it can make doing business more fun and easy when you have a blueprint that gives you the ability to do what you are passionate about, knowing the full scope of how you can accomplish your vision.

A good business plan can be a highly effective tool to manage your business. Write the plan, make it plain and use it as a road map—a blueprint of the strategy to get to your destination of massive business success.

There are several components of a well-crafted business plan, all of which are essential to the full design of the plan. These consist of the vision, the research to support your decision about reaching your target market, the results of your efforts that bring in revenue, the operational strategy and the final step—managing the revenue. All of this represents the road map, the blueprint of the journey to your destination called "massive success."

The Overall Strategy

A business plan is the game plan—the strategy—for operating your business. It will reveal just how good or how weak your idea, product or service is. The act of writing it will often trigger questions that you generally will not think about otherwise. Your answers need to be clear, concise and complete.

Your business plan must state who you are as a company, your mission and your financial goals. You want to be clear about the business you are in and how you will generate revenue. You want to include the details of your market, your competition, your plan for reaching your customers, your plan for generating income and your plan for using and paying vendors and employees. Many people think that marketing and advertising go together. While they do to some extent, they are very different things. Marketing speaks to how you will reach out to *touch* your potential clients, or reach out to *pull* your potential clients. Advertising is one way to reach out to touch or possibly pull your clients. More importantly, it is how you can stay in the forefront of your potential clients who are not ready to do business with you yet.

When creating your market strategy, research and understand how your competition has been successful and determine if a similar strategy would be useful for you. If so, incorporate it into your plan. It is easier to model what has been successful rather than reinvent the wheel. The value is in not having to invest the same amount of time testing something to find out if it is going to work or not. The value in researching is determining if something has worked, how well it has worked and if you can duplicate it successfully. You must, however, also define your target market.

Let's talk about 'target market' because I can hear some of you answering the question, "Who is your target market?" with an answer like "Everyone is my target market!" Your target market is the group of people or businesses that you most resonate with—those who will purchase your goods and/or services. Look at your current client base and you will find that several of your clients fall into a similar category of type of person, face, skin, body structure or business. This similarity can help you as an existing business to identify your target market, and—if you are just starting your business—identify the group of people or businesses that you most want to work with because *that* is where your level of expertise or interest is.

Your business plan must define how you will repay any loans. If you do not plan on obtaining any loans during the course of your business, you can bypass this thought process. However, I encourage my clients to think about this in the planning stages, regardless. If you know what lenders look for in order to consider you for a business loan, you can build and grow your business in such a way that if you chose to obtain a loan in the future, you will be prepared and ready.

Understanding what a lender will look for will help you to best identify and manage your business operations. Business operations are a vital part of the success of your business. In fact, they are the infrastructure that can make or break a business. Make sure you are set up appropriately to manage the processes and systems of how your business will operate, including managing clients, vendors and employees, as well as paying yourself. Work with a coach or consultant if you need processes and systems set up, or if you need them reviewed to see if you could be more efficient in your daily business operations.

If you are a direct sales or multi-level marketing business who has a back office provided for you, you still need a business operations system. You want to record who you are marketing to and how. You want to know how many clients came from which marketing or advertising effort. Many of my clients who are in a direct sales business do not understand that you should have a business bank account. You will want to manage your business like a business and use a business name, even if you are a sole proprietorship.

The Parts of the Plan

Executive summary. This is no more than a two-page summary that describes your plan from start to finish. It provides a complete, concise overall view of what your business is about, who your target market is, how you are different from your competition, how you will conduct business, how you will generate income and how you will manage the operations and finances of the business. Write it so it shows a clear view of how you will get from your conceptual idea—or the place you are now—to your final destination using your vision of success. Briefly state the company objectives, mission and success factors. The following sections of the business plan will provide an opportunity to discuss each area in detail.

Business objectives. This section is the first of the detailed sections of the business plan and focuses on the structure, history and vision of the company. Here you describe how your business will be successful. Be sure to mention how your expertise, coupled with your passion, will be key success factors. You will be sure to give a complete picture of who you are and why you are doing your business when you discuss your business objectives.

Products or services offered. In this section, you describe the products or services you are offering. If you are offering products, explain how you will manufacture the products or how you will acquire parts or full items for inventory and sale. Know how your competition works their business, if possible, so you can compare yourself to them and speak to how cost effectively you are manufacturing your products. Give some information about your delivery process—whether you are going to drop-ship or hand-deliver or some other method—and the reason this method of delivery is best for you.

If you are offering services, describe your expertise and how you will deliver these services to your customers. Make sure you mention how your products fit your target customers' needs and desires. When I designed the business plan for my business, I addressed the services offered and then spoke about the entire process as if I were looking at a flow chart. It gave a complete picture of what a client might experience with each of the services I offer so they or a lender would know exactly what they could expect.

Marketing strategy. In this section, you want to expand on your marketing strategy and talk about the industry and the statistics that support your position about how your products or services meet customers' wants and needs. You want to describe:

• The features and benefits of the products or services you will be delivering to the market place

- Your target customers
- Your competition and how you are different from them
- Your pricing strategy and why it is the right pricing strategy for you
- How you will advertise, brand and promote yourself
- Your sales forecast
- Your key risk factors and milestones

This portion of the plan will describe why your business will benefit prospective and existing clients and how you will grow your business. It will outline the fact that you know your competitors and show how you are different. It will show that you know in advance what your risks are and how you will mitigate them, as well as key milestones that will indicate growth, or when you want to consider changing direction—even if it is only a slight change—by adding a new product, moving to a larger space, or by adding an employee.

Operational plan. Here is where you focus on how you will operate the business. If you are selling products, explain how you will handle a customer from the time they are interested in placing an order through ordering and receiving their product. Include information about how you will handle them to develop recurring business.

If you are offering services, describe how you will manage the customer relationship from the time they express interest in your services through contracting for your services and beyond. Include how you will develop recurring business from existing customers and referrals.

Management and organization. In this section, describe how the business is structured and how it will be managed. If you have staff, define who has oversight of what aspects of the business. If you do not have staff, discuss how your management process meets industry standards and best practices. You should include such things as required education, continuing education, licenses and insurance. Describe who your business advisors are and how they are expected to contribute to the business' success. There are a few people every business owner should consider having as an advisor group and who are you are able to connect with quickly if needed— your attorney, accountant, a business coach or consultant, and a business mentor. With this type of structure for your advisor group, you are sure to be a success.

This is also where you will add any other anticipated issues that could impact the business, such as when you might need a capital infusion, a grant, an angel investor or loan funding.

There is strength in the relationships you build with your clients and your capital money sources. You will build them even more when you are building your business according to a strategy laid out in your business plan. A business coach or mentor can help you design short-term goals and remain accountable for your goals. They will help you celebrate your accomplishments. It is important to acknowledge and celebrate each of your milestone accomplishments while you are on your journey to success, and to share your plan, your vision and your goals.

Financial plan. This is the current financial status of the business. Include details about your personal financials if the business' structure is a sole proprietorship or partnership. If the business is incorporated or an LLC, details of the financials of the entity are essential. (See "The Ten Commandments of Small Business Success" by Nancy Lewellen on page 61.) Details of the start-up expenses, how the business was capitalized, cash flow projections and all financial assumptions are outlined in this section. It is in this section that you describe loans, grants or investor funds. If any funds are used that must be repaid, include information about the repayment (when, how long you will provide for repayment, etc.) This section should be fair, realistic and match your income in the projections.

Appendix. This section will contain information about any references used throughout the business plan and the list and location of any reports, financial statements, charts and graphs that are not already embedded in the body of the business plan.

Style and Substance

Once you have written the details in the business plan, go back and add the elements that will give it style without compromising the substance. This will ensure you have the winning edge. Again, make sure your message is clear and concise, and your facts are correct.

Using applicable analogies and metaphors that will be good examples to show the success you want to see in your business is recommended. Do not use terms that are too industry-specific. If a lay-person will need you to explain a particular term, using a more generic term will allow you to be descriptive enough to be understood. For example, if you are a dermatologist and your target market is people with a rare skin problem, provide the problem's clinical name, then describe it in lay terms and use laymen's terms in any further discussion about how you help this type of client. The reader will know exactly what you are talking about without feeling alienated, especially if you are seeking grant or loan funding.

As you write your plan, remember, you are the expert, and your business is delivering the best products or services. Obtain quotes from other industry experts to use throughout the plan that support what or why you are doing what you are doing. However, keep them to a minimum. You want these statements located in the plan where they will have the most impact. Choose those key places carefully.

Wrap It Up!

Think with the end in mind as you are reviewing your plan. Make sure you have integrated the compelling statements and stories that will cause readers to want to do business with you or to help you.

Create your business plan with all the elements discussed, and you will have mastered the art of writing a winning business plan. Do the things you include in your plan. Have a support structure that can help you stay accountable, stay on course, continue to implement new ideas, celebrate your work throughout the journey and be a part of the cheering when you reach the milestone successes you have dreamed of. When you have reached your destination called "massive success," invite all of your clients, associates, friends and family to celebrate with you. It will have been because of all of their efforts, along with your own, that you will have been such a huge success. Thank them all!

Special *Woman Entrepreneur Extraordinaire* Offer

If you are interested in having Lynn help you to complete a business plan, or in attending one of her workshops and completing a business plan for yourself, visit her website for a schedule of upcoming workshops and register using Discount Code "WEE2011."

V. LYNN HAWKINS
Skyhawk Enterprises

Empowering individuals and businesses to succeed

(408) 758-8868
lynn@skyhawkenterprisesonline.com
www.skyhawkenterprisesonline.com

Silicon Valley, California, business coach, consultant and strategist V. Lynn Hawkins is no stranger to entrepreneurship. She spent the first 25 years of her career running her own successful companies within the corporate structure before deciding to dedicate her work to helping others achieve business success.

Lynn is a business coach, consultant and founder of the Business Empowerment Networking Group, a monthly business networking group focused on business success through coaching. She educates business owners about strategies and methodologies to grow their businesses. Her coaching and consulting services help her clients make more money, increase sales and profits, master time management, achieve their goals and balance their lives. Lynn is passionate about seeing people live a life of abundance. She is committed to spreading positivity and light throughout the world through the work she does.

A frequent speaker, Lynn uses her knowledge and experience to provide high-value, small business resources for her clients. She has facilitated numerous personal development and business coaching workshops and seminars and has served on a variety of panels relating to small business management and development.

Communicating Your Personal Brand
Stand Out with Distinction!
By Melanie Fitzpatrick, CDC, Associate AICI

*I*n today's world, creating and expressing your personal brand is a definitive way to drive your business to greater heights. In leaner economic times, when business opportunities are less abundant, presenting a strong and distinct brand of your services or products is critical to winning new business.

Have you been wondering why your coaching practice is slower than you would prefer, or the sales of your product or services continue to remain flat? Perhaps you have increased the number of your speaking engagements, networking events and virtual exposure without netting the results you expected. You may be in need of some distinction! It may be your *message*—not your *efforts*—that are preventing the growth and financial recognition you require in order to thrive. When you define and continuously express a unique, clear and consistent message of your personal brand to your targeted audience, you stand to gain:

- Recognition as a specialist or an expert

- Increased earnings

- Loyalty and referrals from clients

- Recognition as a thought leader

- Distinction by standing out

Creating a Personal Brand Statement

Your personal brand is best defined as who you uniquely are, what you are known for and how you are perceived in your personal and business life. While we all innately make a statement about who we are and what we value, when it comes to your business, you want to consciously guide this message, so it powerfully conveys how exceptional you are.

Identifying and shaping your message into an effective purpose statement will aide you in building your brand distinction. Knowing and articulating what makes you and your product or service incomparable positions you to be viewed as compelling and communicates a standout message.

> *"What makes you unique, makes you successful."*
> —William Aruda, American author

Your personal brand statement (PBS) communicates your unique capabilities and promise of value. How do you uncover your PBS? By exploring your passions, purpose and vision.

The best way to discover your purpose is to identify what you are most passionate about. As a dream coach, I recommend my clients do the following exercise to open the pathway of insight to their innate purpose.

Take some quiet time away from all your obligations and recall three or four memories of times or situations where you felt alive, exhilarated, peaceful or blissfully content. Have a journal handy and write down these memories.

Next, find the similarities among these memories. It could be words or phrases that resonate deeply or a common theme. Collect them and see if you can write a short phrase with them.

Here is an example of how this exercise worked for one of my clients. Her words distilled from her passion memories were: celebrate, teaching, risk-taking. She discovered her purpose is to celebrate life while teaching in high-risk scenarios. She is now an outdoor adventurer and created a company that teaches rock-climbing skills to individuals and leads corporate team-building events in the wilderness. This fits perfectly into her vision of how she wants to live her life. She created the company to suit her passion and purpose.

Your purpose unfolds from an *introspective* process, and passion flows from the heart. Your vision, however, is more of an *outward* view that is cultivated from your values. How you want to be of service to the world is based on your passion, purpose and skillset. In some cases, you may not have the skillset to serve your purpose and vision and will have to get training.

My outdoor adventure client researched her competition to fully understand their strengths, weaknesses, service offerings and price compared to her offerings and attributes. She formed this personal brand statement to express her uniqueness from other outdoor adventure schools: "I lead individuals and corporate teams to unexplored places within by exposing them to amazing heights in the safest and most challenging way, doing what I love."

Be creative and keep your statement concise while including your target market, passion, skills and vision. Write a couple of versions and test them out on trusted sources and see which one speaks to you the most. Remember, the key element here is defining your unique promise of value and making it memorable by making it distinctive.

- What are your strengths and attributes that make you the better choice than others?

- List your attributes, special talents and abilities.

- Connect your attributes and your promise of value.

- Transform your attributes into assets.

This is how you differentiate your services or products from the competition and stand out! It is your most powerful message and should be consistently and congruently communicated to your target audience.

You know how you will be of service to the world in your distinctive way and have created your PBS that acts as your compass while navigating toward your goals. Now, you can build brand strength by aligning your verbal and nonverbal messages with your PBS. A congruency in the key components of visual identity, vocal quality and body language develops credibility.

Your Visual Brand

A strong component of your brand package is the visual presentation of yourself. Your professional appearance must communicate the attributes of your personal brand and be appropriate to your target audience. If you are forward thinking and creative, you will want your style to reflect those qualities, perhaps by dressing with an urban chic skirt suit in medium-rich tones, leather dress boots and a colorful scarf. If your message and style is a conservative, yet approachable one, you might wear an elegantly tailored pantsuit in a soft pastel or muted color, high-end minimalist jewelry and two-inch heeled pumps.

If you are wondering if you have developed the right style and level of dress appropriate for your message, consider your customers. Are they individuals, small businesses or major corporations? In what industries do you develop business? In the world of finance and banking, dress is usually conservative and traditional with business-professional or power-professional suiting. In the arts and marketing industries, a creative, business casual or business professional works. In corporate America, you will find a mix of classic and traditional styles in business professional and power professional along with business casual, depending on the level of person and department with which you interface.

Jeffery J. Fox said it best in *How to Become a RAINMAKER,* published by Hyperion in 2000, "Your dress should signal confidence, success, expertise, sensitivity, professionalism and attention to detail."

You can influence the outcome of any event by becoming strategic about your professional style presentation. Use the Style Guide on page 113 to help you determine your professional style type and characteristics that best suit your brand statement. It also shows you the appropriate level of business attire that will create that all-important winning presence.

Consider these major influencers of style:

Color. Finding colors that look good on your skin tone, eye and hair color is essential. Often, we are naturally drawn to colors that work best for us. Colors convey expression and meaning. When using the Color Communication Chart found on page 112, you will notice that both nouns and adjectives are used to describe the meanings that a color conveys. For example, red is a *high-energy* color that expresses *excitement.* Make sure the colors you choose send the message that fits with your brand attributes. For example, if you need to build trust and credibility, wear medium tones of the color blue to convey this message. Keep this in mind when creating your visual identity system for your website, business colors, logo, handouts and business cards. (See "Quick Tips to Put Your Website to Work" by Tammy Tribble on page 177.)

Power colors are the deepest tone of a specific color and impart the highest level of influence. The color chart can also be used to identify the power colors right for you when you need to ramp up the intensity!

COLOR COMMUNICATION ●●○○● CHART ●●○○○

color	message
red ★	excitement, desire, energy, power, intense, risk, energy, strength
orange	enthusiasm, determination, energy, vitality, strength, productive, warmth
yellow	joy, bright, positive, visionary, idealism, futuristic, approachable
green ★	natural, environmental, healthy, calming, fertile, renewal
blue ★ᶜ	credible, trusting, loyal, authority, tranquility, peaceful, stable
purple ★	wealthy, royalty, luxury, mystery, spirituality, wisdom
brown ★	earthy, dependable, stable, reliable, endurance, simplicity
black ★ᶜ	power, sophistication, wealth, anonymity, authority, formality
grey	reliability, security, intelligence, modesty, conservative, dignity

★ power color in the richest tone   ᶜ best power color choice

Fit. This pertains to how a garment conforms or clings to your body type. If you are not a regular store size, then buy the size that best fits your body and have it tailored. Ill-fitting clothing will sabotage your positive impression. It is a glaring mistake, as it says, "I am not good with details," or "How I look doesn't matter."

A great-fitting suit can enhance any body type and make you feel incredible, maybe even unstoppable. Find a good tailor. He or she may become your new best friend!

Style. Match your personal style of dress to the audience, whether you are doing a customer presentation, a speaking event, networking or attending a training class. Using the Style Guide below can help you decide what level of business dress is appropriate.

- **Power professional.** Matching pant or skirt suit in your power color

- **Business professional.** Dressing in separates that are a mix of color and prints for jacket and skirt, jacket and pants, and dresses; your jacket is your statement of authority

- **Business casual.** Dressing in separates that are a mix of color and prints; a jacket is not always needed if your look is polished yet relaxed

Style GUIDE

style	characteristics	appropriateness for business	classification
classical/traditional	elegant, tailored, conservative	5	power professional
dramatic	fashion forward, urban, chic, theatrical flare	5	power professional
alluring	glamorous, sexy, dramatic	1	casual
casual/active	athletic, natural, relaxed	2	casual/business casual
romantic	feminine, soft, delicate, detailed	4	business professional/business casual
creative	artsy, playful, funky	3	business professional/business casual

Hair. Your haircut must reflect a modern, attractive style. A good hairdresser will work with the texture of your hair and face shape to provide a professional cut that looks appropriate. If you have had the same hairstyle for five or more years, it is time for a change!

Makeup. Wear it! Women who do earn incomes that are twenty percent to thirty percent higher than those who do not according to Sherry Maysonave in her enlightening guidebook *Casual Power,* published by Bright Books in 1999. Makeup hides flaws and enhances your beauty! Its effect says that you care about yourself and pay attention to detail. If you are a minimalist, wear at least mascara and lipstick. If you like makeup and wear it regularly, keep it to a day look and save the smoky, sexy eyes for evening. Strike the proper balance that is neither too heavy nor too light. Your goal is to strive to look natural, yet enhanced.

Vocal Communication

Your presentation skills are paramount for communicating and supporting the attributes of your brand. Vocal skills must have effective quality, energy, volume and diction.

Audience. To whom are you speaking? Are they schoolteachers or bankers, laborers or nurses? How do you want to be perceived? Likeable, authoritative, trustworthy? Use their language or buzzwords in your speech, and they will perceive you as an insider. This will help you create a bond with them and signal you are familiar with their business or industry. Avoid slang words, racial or vulgar jokes and political opinions unless you are in politics. By all means, include humor appropriately! Speakers are appreciated and remembered most for being funny. This is a gift you will leave with your audience.

Energy. The key thing about energy is controlling it and matching the energy in the room. Nerves can derail your energy and cause your vocal tempo to speed up, your pitch to rise and the amount of vocal fillers, such as "and," "um" and "uh," to increase. It can also cause you to pace back and forth.

This is where effective pre-speech preparation will come into play. Practice deep breathing five to ten minutes before your presentation or speech. Close your eyes, breathe in through your nose on a count of 12 and exhale through your mouth on a count of 12. Repeat as many times as needed and add a self-affirming mantra.

Set an intention as you visualize the most positive outcome by seeing yourself in front of the audience speaking with control, confidence and command! Customize a pre-speech ritual that works for you and use it every time. This is what professional speakers do.

Volume. How loud or soft you speak is contingent on the size and space of the room and whether or not you are using a microphone. Consider the event, as well.

- At a networking event where you are speaking to people one-on-one, keep volume conversational. If you have a naturally loud or husky voice, soften it.

- If you are at a meeting and have the opportunity to stand and give your elevator pitch, project to the person farthest from you. Speak slowly, smile and make eye contact with people.

- If you are speaking at an event and are not given a microphone, project your voice to the person farthest from you while breathing deeply from your diaphragm. It will sound loud to you—this will be your cue that you are speaking loud enough to be heard! Projecting the voice on a well-supported breath will enable you to speak for longer periods without losing your voice.

- If you are speaking with a headset or a handheld microphone, watch your P's and S's. P's can sound explosive, and S's can have a hissing sound. If you get feedback, adjust the distance of the microphone away from your mouth.

Pitch and tone. Pitch is the height or depth of the sound of your speaking voice. Tone is the quality of your voice, whether is it is nasally, breathy, husky or shrill. For the most pleasant sound, speak in the mid- to lower-pitch of your voice.

If you are wondering what type of voice quality you have, use a voice recorder, such as a cell phone or mp3 player, and recite a couple paragraphs from a book or magazine. Play it back and listen to it. Ask a trusted friend to comment on your sound. If your voice is too husky or low, practice with your voice slightly raised until that sound is familiar and comfortable to you. Use the opposite technique if your speaking voice is too high, consciously lower it and practice with the recorder until you can feel and hear the difference.

Enunciation. Speaking with excellent diction and correct pronunciation reinforces your credibility. If you have a regional or international accent, soften it, so you can be understood. Practice with the recorder while over articulating your consonants and endings of each word.

Body Language

People's gestures and behavior give away their true intentions. Fifty-five percent of the overall impression we make is comprised of appearance and body language. Becoming consciously aware of what your body is expressing is critical to sending a message that is congruent with your brand message.

Some pointers for body language:

• Tall erect posture communicates confidence.

- Direct eye contact establishes trust.

- Smiling welcomes and makes someone feel important.

- Arms should hang naturally to show openness and ease. Crossed arms show a mind that is closed to what is being said.

- Open palms show you have nothing to hide and should always be visible, especially when speaking professionally. Closed palms impart aggression.

- Excessive body or hand movements will detract from what you are saying.

- Feet communicate direction. When talking one-on-one with someone, if the feet point away from you, this is a signal he or she wants to leave.

As you become more mindful of your body language, you can begin to use these nonverbal cues to communicate more effectively and get the reactions you are seeking!

Refining and presenting your message and services with power and passion will clearly put you a notch above everyone else. Remember, passion sells! When you align the strategic elements of your brand and communicate with clarity and distinction, you will be clicking on all cylinders and will be unstoppable!

Present yourself as a powerfully put-together package. Empower that all-important first impression and consciously convey who you are and what your authentic value is.

Special *Woman Entrepreneur Extraordinaire* Offer

Visit my web site at www.empoweringimages.com and request a free consultation to get you on your way!

MELANIE FITZPATRICK, CDC, Associate AICI

Speaker, Author, Coach, Trainer

(412) 736-6067

melanie@empoweringimages.com

www.empoweringimages.com

Melanie Fitzpatrick brings a wealth of experience and knowledge to her clients as a sought-after business coach. In addition to her passion for image and presentation, she has extensive vocal, stage and on-camera training and experience in the performing arts industry. She has twenty-five years of corporate experience, managing a multi-million dollar portfolio as a national account manager. She loves to work with highly motivated individuals with a desire to grow and expand their personal brand and business.

Inspired to follow her own dreams of leading others to discover and develop their greater potential, Melanie became certified as a Dream Coach® through Dream University™ and is a 360 Reach Brand Analyst. As a life coach she engages her clients with a highly effective program focused on purpose development and vision realization.

Melanie resides in Pittsburgh, Pennsylvania, with her family. In her free time, she enjoys cycling, skiing and cultural events. She is a volunteer coach at Dress for Success, a national organization that promotes economic independence for disadvantaged women by helping them gain and retain meaningful employment. She is an affiliate member of National Speakers Association®, Pittsburgh, and a member of Pittsburgh Professional Women's Network.

Your Invisible Edge in Business
By Yvette Ervin

We have all seen her. She is the one who stands out from the rest. It is not just her dress, fresh hairstyle or air of mystery. She actually looks successful and pulled together. Something tells you that she is good at what she does. That "something" is the *invisible edge!* The look stops traffic like a red light. The invisible edge is that certain *jen ne sais quoi*—an indefinable charm that makes people notice you. Every woman entrepreneur needs an invisible edge in business because you have to create and use every advantage possible, especially in this difficult economy.

You want to make a clear and indisputable message with your image. You want to say, "This is who I am with all my beliefs, values and background. I'm competent, successful and approachable in my business." You demonstrate value.

It is all about being yourself and designing a visual message that speaks to your core audience before you say a word. You are the author, messenger and ambassador of your image—your personal and professional brand. Your most powerful resource is controlling your image.

Remember, having a charismatic image is not always about being pretty, having the best designer gear or being the sharpest woman in the room. It is about showing potential clients who you are by being honest and open about your true nature and motives.

One of my clients, Margo, wanted to become a color expert and authority to the international hair industry. She is 5-feet 9-inches tall, weighs 300 pounds and is an eccentric colorist extraordinaire. She has been a trendsetter in her industry for years, and she's looking to become the next household name in the world of hair.

At our first meeting, I learned that Margo was okay with her weight and her "creative" side. After all, it's a big part of who she is. Her health is good, and she is comfortable in her own skin. She needed help with etiquette, she dressed like a 48-year-old cheerleader, and she did not command a presence that is worthy of her skills and level of professionalism.

Margo exuded an image of "large, but not in charge." Consequently, she had trouble with things like obtaining sponsorship from hair care companies, being chosen as a member of national styling teams and getting interviews since the press seldom were interested in her even though she had won several coveted awards.

After working with Margo, she has "spread her wings." She was featured on the cover of a popular industry trade magazine. She wears a chic, edgy, short, colorful hairstyle and tailored pantsuits, which have become her signature dress. Margo would not be Margo without her eccentricity, and her personality is always present in the form of bold accessories, ever-changing hair, long nails and flawless makeup. Margo's time with an etiquette and speech coach has also paid off. She looks happy and approachable. When you see her, you know she belongs in the winner's circle. Her skills and talent are apparent on the outside. She is more sought after and more successful while staying true to who she is. Margo has the invisible edge "big time."

When defining your invisible edge, you never need permission to be yourself, so work it!

Seven Seconds to Impact

Let's look at the seven-second rule. According to Kathryn Volin, author of the book *Buff and Polish,* published by Virtualbookworm.com in 1999, within a time span of seven seconds, you have already decided whether or not you like someone you have encountered—and *they* have made that same judgment about *you!* She goes on to write, "While they're making judgments about you in seven seconds, within thirty seconds they've made at least eleven assumptions about you."

You only have a few seconds to communicate who you are. Potential clients read your image before they get to know how amazing you are. First impressions in business relationships are critical. People consciously or unconsciously label you as "likable" or "unlikable." Every other interaction is an extension of this judgment and is filtered through these filters. While opinions can change, the power of that first impression is forever and can stay in someone's mind for a long time. (See "Communicating Your Personal Brand" by Melanie Fitzpatrick on page 107.)

> *"If it looks like a duck, quacks like a duck, it must be a duck."*
> —Author Unknown

I know many women who find themselves straddling more worlds than one. Some of us are moms, businesswomen, artists and caregivers to our aging parents. At times, defining ourselves through our authentic image may feel strange or confusing because we are so many things to so many people. We feel at odds with who we are and struggle with how we define our image both to ourselves and the rest of the world.

Are you the one who says, "I need to get my look together," or "She must have lots of time to put herself together, but I don't"? Do you ever use this excuse, "I'll begin to do that [get fit, get a new wardrobe, get a new hair style] when I have the [time, money and so on]"?

Do you believe you cannot afford to focus on creating your image?

You cannot afford not to.

Selling without Selling

Clients believe what they see. It is wonderful to have an impressive website or other company branding. However, your physical image must be in alignment with your business culture and brand, or you create a disconnect.

In our fast-paced world, many opportunities are won or lost based on your image. It is a matter of landing the contract on the spot or not being considered as a serious contender for coveted clients or key associations.

I like to call the invisible edge "selling without selling." Remember, we are constantly selling ourselves. Whether you are going for a huge ticket sale, securing an appointment, selling a soft service, fund-raising or enrolling a team in your extraordinary vision, the invisible edge is your secret weapon.

We are not clones or slaves to our professions. Having your own business gives you freedom to "do it your way." Regardless of how great your service or product is, your image is definitely something to consider whether you are transitioning into entrepreneurship or are a seasoned professional with great accounts and clients. The physical must be in sync with the actual business purpose. When they are not aligned, it is off putting and confusing to potential clients and business associates.

Five Steps to the Invisible Edge

You can have whatever you want. It is all about what is important in your business. You want instant recognition to attract your ideal clients and have them come to you. What makes people choose between two well-qualified businesses? What is the invisible edge that tips their decision? *It is your message, your visual elements and your charisma.* It is a nonverbal communication that causes clients to say, "I feel like you represent who we are and where we are headed." Here are five steps to help give you this invisible edge.

Step One: Prioritize. The first thing is deciding what is important to you. What do you wish to be known for to your clients or audience? Having a clear-cut image and brand is crucial, especially if you are new in business or are transitioning from a job or another career.

An image of credibility, professionalism and value says, "I pay attention to details. I'm working for you." This image is part of my company culture. I communicate this message whether I am in a meeting, having lunch with a client or attending a weekend retreat. My image screams, "I live, breath and sleep this image. This is a piece of who I am." (See "Exemplifying Authenticity and Excellence as an Entrepreneur" by Lisa Centamore Sinkiewicz on page 1.)

- Be clear why you are in business in the first place and create a vision of where you see yourself in five years.

- What do you want your clients to feel from their experience of working with you?

- Make a list of how you add value to your clients.

Step Two: Know your target market. This point is simple, yet key, in creating an effective self-image in your business.

To whom are you talking?

This is the million-dollar question. Imagine you see your latest client, Lisa, coming out of Starbucks®. You have been trying to get her on the phone for days, and, suddenly, there she is. You call out Lisa's name, but she does not respond. You call her again. A few bystanders turn around, yet no one answers to the name "Lisa." You think, "Why isn't she answering me?"

The answer: Your new client does not hear you because her name is not "Lisa." It's "Justine"—different name, big result.

You have to know your clients and potential clients—down to the smallest detail! The more you know about them, the more they will respond to you with familiarity and warmth. This is a critical component of your invisible edge. People need to be able to recognize you, even when you are not in front of them.

You recognize the Golden Arches® from the freeway even when you are traveling sixty-five-plus miles per hour. When you think of sporting gear, Nike® comes to mind. McDonalds® and Nike have the invisible edge!

- When people think of the products or services you provide, do they think of you? When they do, they understand your company culture based on what you represent to them. They get you. You have the invisible edge.

- Your target market is your community. Make it a point to see them not just as your audience but also as your extended circle of friends.

- Speak to their needs.

- Think like your target audience. Buy what they buy, do what they do, live in their shoes. Know them better than they know themselves.

Step Three: Make it seem effortless. Make it look like you are comfortable in your own skin, and, yes, I always look like this. You have heard women say, "Oh, this is nothing. I just threw it together." Not true. It takes effort to look effortless. The only way it will be effortless is if you have all the necessary picccs, and you do it until it seems like second nature. The more you know what those pieces are, and the more you work on putting them together, the easier it becomes. In the end, it becomes effortless. It is never about trying hard. (See "Think Like a CEO" by Alice Hinckley on page 37.)

Create time and a budget for you and your personal needs. For example, if you need more time to go to the gym or for regular sessions with your hair stylist, make it a necessary item on your to-do list for your business. Do not put it at the bottom of the list. It is not one of the things you do when you have time.

Keep it simple. Create a formula that works for you and includes two to three different accents. I have a client who hated wearing eyeglasses but made it work for her. Now, every time I see her, she wears the most amazing and stylish frames. She has made it work for her and her personality comes through, which we all love. It has become part of her brand.

In the early stages of my business, I did not have much cash to spend on myself. It seemed like every penny I earned went into the till. I would think to myself, "How can I help empower women when I do not look or feel like I represent what I am selling?" I devised a little secret. I became so resourceful in defining my brand that I didn't even feel like I was creating my invisible edge. After all, I was just doing and being what I always do but applied it to my overall visual.

My formula was based partly on refined tastes, practicality, which my mother instilled in me as a child, and my love of the "what's different." This sums up my invisible edge.

• Get organized.

• Make yourself distinctive. Is there a professional code, demeanor, style or action in your field you must adhere to? Add your own accents, colors or flair. Something that let's others know who you are and makes you unique. No one does you as you do you. This makes it seem effortless and easy. You do not have to try. You just are! Former United States Secretary of State Madeleine Albright always wore a distinctive pin. She became known for this accessory, and a collection of her pins was made into a book.

Step Four: Always put you in the mix. When you put you in the mix, you make your image authentic and unique. There is no text-book or cookie-cutter image makeover. Only one person can do you, and that is you. The great news is this—when you tap into your authentic and unique image, no one can copy it. They can try, but they will not succeed.

Let's look at a few examples. When you see Oprah Winfrey, you know it is she. It is not about her clothes, hair, style of dress or makeup. She presents herself in a way that demonstrates her lifestyle, brand, core values and message. She is what she stands for. These things change only slightly over time. It says to women all over the world, "This is who I am," and the world speaks back and says, "We love you for you—you're real!"

Find something about yourself that you like. Make it part of your identifiable charm. I have a client who loves art and all things creative. She works, lives and thrives in this environment. When meeting potential buyers or investors, she does not try to make them think she is a businessperson by wearing traditional business attire. She is an artist. Her unique aesthetic shines though.

Step Five: Don't switch hit. "Switch hit" is a term I borrowed from baseball. It refers to the player's ability to hit the ball from both the left and the right sides of the plate.

When you switch hit your image, it means you are constantly changing your signature style. This confuses your audience. You can make changes without changing your essence and without changing the signature elements that define you. Your signature elements are things like a hairstyle that suits you, and no one else can quite pull off the way you do.

Actress Audrey Hepburn had a petite frame and wore timeless classics in black. She was, and still is, one of the greatest fashion icons of the twentieth century. With her delicate features and body, she was the muse for fashion designer Givenchy. Even today, she is still recognized as the essence of classic American chic. No one has ever epitomized the "little black dress" as she did in *Breakfast at Tiffany's.*

- Decide the key components of your image. Approach your image as if you are making a delicious meal. It must say who and what you are, ring true and authentic and be pleasing to the eyes. Your ideal clients have fine tastes and cannot wait to experience your offerings.

- Make subtle adjustments without selling out. It is important to constantly add new tweaks here and there while remaining true to who you are. Fads, trends and fashions come and go. Make who you are a constant reminder of your company's core message.

Do not follow the crowd. Just do you!

Action Steps

Your invisible edge is the secret to entrepreneurial success. With it, you do not need to compete for business because no one offers exactly what you do in exactly your way.

Be unique. Be you. Be successful!

Special *Woman Entrepreneur Extraordinaire* Offer

Are you ready to take yourself and take your business to the next level by creating your signature invisible edge? When you confirm a Beauty Full of Color Skype® session, you can bring a friend or family member *to the same session FREE.* Contact me (510) 575-1705 or email contact@beautyfullofcolor.com about this Two-for-One Skype consultation.

YVETTE ERVIN
Beauty Evolutionist, Image Specialist,
Author and Speaker

Image—The Invisible Edge
Beauty Full of Color™

(510) 575-1705
contact@beautyfullofcolor.com
www.beautyfullofcolor.com

Yvette Ervin is a beauty evolutionist, image specialist and the founder of *Beauty Full of Color*™. She doesn't just consult with women. She *empowers* women to create an image that exudes confidence, individuality and charisma. Yvette's successful modeling career kicked off a 14-year international career as an insider in the exciting world of fashion and beauty. She has worked as a stylist, makeup artist, editor and producer for several international magazines and productions.

Her successful career working with industry giants has greatly influenced Yvette's approach to image and the modern woman. She is on a mission to help business women refine and celebrate their "inner celebrity" by uncovering their personal invisible edge that helps catapult success and satisfaction. Yvette has the unique ability of unearthing your distinctive brand and giving her clients "out-of-the-box" changeover sessions that transform them from the inside out.

A lively and dynamic speaker, Yvette leads fun and interactive workshops that empower women to identify their personal invisible edge and utilize it to their advantage. Her motto is, "Every difference, every oddity, we color it beautiful."

Customer Service Cuts through Competition

By Sheri Brunnquell

*C*ompetition. The word strikes fear in the hearts of many entrepreneurs. The feeling of competition can make you want to quit before you even begin.

Do you feel anxious about businesses who offer the same product or service as you do?

Do you wonder if you can compete with businesses that have a bigger marketing budget, an ideal storefront location, more experienced management or more resources?

If you are stuck in the idea you cannot succeed because of competition, it is time to change your perspective. As an entrepreneur, you must believe there is an abundance of customers ready to accept what you have to offer once you connect with them.

Your *real competition* is not other people or businesses. It is the infinite number of choices your clients have for spending their money and time. When they are ready to invest, how do you ensure they choose you?

Customer service is giving those with whom you do business a feeling of satisfaction, of being valued and of being taken care of by you and your team. Customer service is the key for retaining your clients and gaining new ones. It eliminates the anxiety you feel that others have an advantage over you. In fact, extraordinary customer service is so often overlooked that those who do it well have the overwhelming advantage.

One of the biggest mistakes entrepreneurs make when building their businesses is to try to compete with others by cutting prices or by having aggressive sales. They may take a monetary loss in their business, thinking that they will adjust prices later to recoup. When you use this strategy, you are running your business out of fear—fear that you do not have what it takes to compete. Instead of *devaluing* what you offer, give your customers *more*. Treat them as the important part of your business they are.

Begin branding yourself through the sterling customer experience you offer, and your customers will keep coming back to you. Not only will they return, they will bring their friends with them! (See the chapter "Break Free to Six Figures" by Georgina Sweeney on page 209.)

Define What Keeps *You* as a Customer

Developing a customer service mission statement is the first step in offering amazing customer service. As you read on, you may want to jot down ideas or keep a small notebook with your thoughts on customer service.

> *"Do what you do so well that they will want*
> *to see it again and bring their friends."*
> —Walt Disney, American visionary

Think about the businesses you have used. Is there a business you will use even if you have to pay a little more? Have you ever stopped using a business even though the price was right because you did not enjoy the overall experience?

Choose a model of customer service that reflects your own customer service values. If it is important to you, it is most likely important to your clients as well. Make a list of companies that treat you well and jot down examples of what they do to make you feel like a valued customer.

It may be hard to pinpoint an event that made you feel valued. You may just know you like being there. I urge you, however, to start noting instances that make you feel special. This is important in refining your own customer service practices. Businesses that make you feel valued may know you by name, may remember a certain style or item you like, may call you when they are having a special event. They are polite and happy to see you when you come to buy— even when you are just browsing.

List some key adjectives you would like your customers to use when they describe your business to a friend. Post those adjectives where you see them daily and often check yourself across all aspects of your business to ensure that you are living up to your ideal image. When my customers think of me, I want them to think "elegant, innovative, knowledgeable and helpful." I strive to carry that brand throughout my marketing materials and with every interaction I have.

Demonstrate Your Commitment to Customer Care from the Very First Contact

From every phone call you receive to Internet connections to face-to-face interactions, your mission is to let your customer know you *care about their consumer needs.*

The initial customer contact may come from a phone inquiry. A potential client may have found out about your business from a friend or an Internet search or may have met you briefly. He or she knows a bit about you and what you do.

Many clients have been lost because of poor phone etiquette. Potential clients are calling because they are curious about your products or services. They are a *warm* lead that has not been won over. This is their first impression of how you will treat them.

Is your phone greeting message aligned with your key adjectives? If you want your clients to know you are professional, creative or energetic, does your voicemail message reflect that? Here is my phone greeting:

Hello. You've reached Sheri, the Silver Gal, Brunnquell sterling silver independent representative. I'm sorry I've missed your call but please leave me a message, and I'll get back to you right away. Have a sterling day!

Many entrepreneurs publish their home phone number, so they can be reached at any time. Is your home voicemail message appropriate for potential clients? If there is a possibility someone else may pick up that call at home, it may be wise to use a separate business line only you answer.

Make certain your voice mailbox is working and has room for new messages. Most importantly, always return phone calls in a timely manner. Make it your goal to respond to all phone inquiries within twenty-four business hours.

When you have the opportunity to speak with someone, minimize distracting background noises, such as children playing—or arguing—the television or radio in the background and outside noises like a lawn mower, leaf blower or barking dog.

Instead of a phone call, your customer may browse your website or send you an email. Make sure your email address appears on your business card, your website and all marketing materials. Some entrepreneurs omit the email address on their business cards. They hope to drive potential clients straight to their website. This is not a good practice. You may lose a potential client completely if you make it too hard for them to ask a question about your products or services.

It is best to keep your email address something memorable and easy to spell. It needs to reflect your brand. My name is tricky to spell, so my email address is thesilvergal@me.com. I consistently use "the silver gal" brand, so it is easy to remember. Again, be sure to respond within an acceptable amount of time to your emails, usually within 24 business hours of the email landing in your inbox. Use auto-responders only for vacation alerts or if you will be out of the office and cannot respond promptly.

If you have a storefront, you may attract potential clients as they pass by and want to see what you are about. You want your location to look inviting and clean. Adhere to your posted business hours and offer hours of operation that will appeal to your ideal client. I once wanted to check out a new clothing boutique in a neighborhood I visited occasionally. It looked interesting, and I really wanted to see what was inside. Every time I planned to be in the area, I went a little early or allowed some extra time, so I could stop in. Despite the fact that all the other businesses around it were open for business, I never found this store open. After a few months, the boutique had a closed sign in the window.

"Repetition makes reputation and reputation makes customers."
—Elizabeth Arden, Canadian cosmetics pioneer

Good Customer Service Equals Customer Retention

Once you gain a client, you must continue to provide a level of customer service that makes you stand out from everyone else. Your customers still have all those alternatives that compete for their time and money. Now is the time to show them how much their patronage means to you.

After providing excellent service at your first contact, the next step is to help them remember that you are there. Staying top-of-mind is a huge part of customer service. If you are right there when your customer thinks of calling you, he or she will perceive you as being efficient and on top of your game.

Some entrepreneurs believe a customer thinks of calling them only when the customer needs them. They think that they do not have to check in with their clients on a regular basis because they assume that if their customer needs something, that customer will seek them out. In reality, the customer will often not take action and will find another way to spend his or her time and money. You can greatly increase the number of times your customers come to you if you stay on their radar.

The Internet is an effective and inexpensive way to keep in touch with your customer. Social media sites, such as Facebook®, LinkedIn® and Twitter® help you stay top-of-mind. So is the use of email marketing e-zines. An e-zine is a digital newsletter that brings value-based information to your customers on a frequent, regular basis, such as weekly or monthly. Several reputable companies provide this service. I use Constant Contact®—iContact® and VerticalResponse® are other well-known providers of this service.

Your e-zine is not the place to sell. If you view your e-zine as a way of sharing information and leading your client to make the decision that they need your product or service, you will see results.

E-zines have become widely used, so, as with all your customer contacts, it must represent the image and brand you want to portray. Misspellings, grammar errors and poor writing do not reflect the professional image you want. If the written word is not your strength, consider hiring a writer and virtual assistant to write and distribute your e-zine.

Email marketing services allow you to track your customers' interests as they follow links for more information throughout your content. Use this information to further help your customers get what they need, and you will be an intuitive savvy entrepreneur!

Email marketing also allows you to promote events and remember client birthdays and other special occasions. When you can show your customers you think of them as a valuable part of your business, you will solidify your relationships with them. (See also "It's Not Stalking...It's Follow Up!" by Elizabeth McCormick on page 143.)

Create Unique Experiences for Your Customers

Few entrepreneurs have the luxury of being the only one who offers their products or services. If your customers can find what you offer at a number of businesses, you must give them a reason to always come to you. Creating a unique customer experience differentiates you from others.

In my business as a direct sales representative, my product is the same as that of 35,000 other women across the country. Because my product cannot be different, I have to be the difference. I want to offer my customers something no other representative in my company offers. To do this, I find out what others are doing and go beyond that.

At age 26, Canadian recreational skier Vince Poscente decided to pursue speed skiing competitively. He started training and four years later, he was vying for gold in the Winter Olympics. His key to success: "Don't just do what the competition isn't doing; do what the competition isn't *willing to do.*" This can help you be the difference that sets you apart.

Last year, my company offered a very compelling sales incentive—an all-expenses-paid trip to Spain. In order to earn it, I needed more sales revenue than I had ever sold before. Vince's motto was my key to success.

Memorial Day weekend was coming, and a blockbuster movie was being released. I thought, "What if I could rent out the movie theater and host a private screening for that movie?" My plan was to give a ticket to anyone who purchased $50 of my products.

I almost dismissed the idea as impossible. After all, I did not know what it cost to rent out a theater. I did not know if I could sell $50 purchases to make back my investment. I could have given up. Instead, I called the movie theater, got the cost information, gave them my credit card number and reserved the private screening. Then, I got on the phone and started selling.

It was a huge success! I earned the incentive by playing big and by taking a risk that most would not be willing to do. I also earned the respect and attention of my customers by offering a truly unique experience.

You do not have to spend a lot of money to host a fun event like the one I described above. You do have to use your imagination and ask yourself, "What are others unwilling to do?"

Customer appreciation events are a great way to give back to your clientele, and I recommend hosting quarterly events. You can also cross-promote with another business owner who has a complimentary product or service to offer. Remember, sometimes a small monetary investment within your marketing budget can pay off ten-fold in the following months. In my movie example, I not only had big sales at my movie event, I was able to book five parties and add three, new team members because of my phone calls promoting the event. The movie event by itself would not have gotten me to Spain, but all the consequent business put me over the top.

Is the Customer Always Right?

An occasional customer disagreement is inevitable. We live in an age of entitlement where some may take advantage of those who offer more.

Is the customer always right? The answer is a resounding no! It is in your best interest to listen closely when your customer has a complaint or a request, and then you must stay true to your policies. Do your best to find out what your customer really wants and run your business like a business. Weigh the implications of your response and try to accommodate the customer, when possible. Look at your policies if an issue arises often, and view customer complaints as feedback for improving customer relations. (See the chapter "Think Like a CEO" by Alice Hinckley on page 37.)

There are times when you will have to make a choice between allowing your customer to be right and honoring what you must do as a businesswoman. I have turned down requests for an exchange past my deadline and denied expired special offers. However, I do not leave my customer with a flat no. I will offer to help that person find a buyer for the item they wish to exchange or let them know I will check in with them personally the next time I can help them take advantage of one of my specials. I urge you to resist making snap judgments when dealing with a complaint or an irate customer. You cannot please everyone all the time.

> *"It's important that people should know what you stand for.*
> *It's equally important that they should know*
> *what you won't stand for."*
> —Mary H Waldrip, American author

Sterling Customer Service Starts Now

Revisit your list of adjectives. How do you rate in displaying your values to your customers? Do you have areas that you would like to improve?

You can always take customer service a step further. You may not be able to re-vamp all areas of your customer care at once. Start with your next customer contact and pledge to make every subsequent interaction positive and nurturing. If you have customers who have fallen out of touch, take a little time every day to call them and to reconnect. Conquer your world with a brand of customer service that is unparalleled. Go the distance and enjoy the view. As Hall of Fame® quarterback Roger Staubach once said, "There are no traffic jams along the extra mile."

Special *Woman Entrepreneur Extraordinaire* Offer

Direct sales can be the perfect vehicle for the budding entrepreneur. However, the fear of being "salesy" holds many back. Visit www. thesilvergal.com to download my free guide *Five Steps to Shatter Direct Sales Stigma.*

SHERI BRUNNQUELL
"The Silver Gal"
Silpada Designs Independent
Representative

Jewelry finishes your "look."

(916) 847-6433
thesilvergal@me.com
www.thesilvergal.com

In 2005, Sheri Brunnquell became an "accidental entrepreneur." Looking for a way to juggle family, career and personal "me" time, she found her solution in direct sales as an independent representative with Silpada Designs® Jewelry.

Aspiring to be more than just another salesperson, she learned early in her direct selling career to consider her job to be part of the service, not the sales, industry. She has earned leadership recognition and has spoken for the company on national tele-clinics and at local events. She is consistently in the top one percent for personal sales and leads a team of forty women.

A former teacher, Sheri's love of sharing information has allowed her to train and mentor representatives across the country. She offers her clients a solution in their quest for the perfect look and image and helps her team balance all aspects of their lives as modern-day businesswomen. Her passion is to help women realize their potential by helping them set and accomplish their personal goals. Sheri leads by example. She believes that anything you really want from your business is possible with determination and a positive outlook.

It's Not Stalking...It's Follow Up!
By Elizabeth McCormick

When I started my business, I had to make it work. It was a do-or-die time for me. My part-time, fun-time business while working in a corporate job was now my full-time, pay-the-bills business! I had to be smart about money. I did not have a big budget for advertising and events. What to do?

By improving my follow-through at lower cost networking events, meetings and conferences I was already attending, I *doubled* my business in *one year*. Would you like to double your sales *and* your income in one year? Well, you can.

If you are taking the time to attend networking events and conferences—and you know time is money when you are an entrepreneur—you are investing in yourself and your business. Why aren't you making the most of it?

The solution to these overlooked connections? A solid follow-through plan.

We all have good intentions about following up. We know it is an essential part of building our contacts and businesses. How many entrepreneurs actually follow through? Don't be one of those who does not. Start now and build a solid follow-through plan to make your connections count.

Maybe you already have a follow-up plan that serves your existing clients and helps you gain new business. You are truly exceptional. Just keep an open mind as you read this chapter. You may learn something that could propel your business to a higher level. As technology advances and clients become more savvy, you need to evolve and ensure you provide solutions your clients need.

> *"Everyone has an invisible sign hanging from their neck saying,*
> *'Make me feel important.'*
> *Never forget this message when working with people."*
> —Mary Kay Ash, American, founder Mary Kay®

What Is Follow Through?

At first, it seems simple. Do what you say and say what you mean. To an entrepreneur, follow through separates you from your competitors. This service to your clients takes you up a notch and differentiates you in the marketplace.

Start with your existing clients.

If you do not have a plan to follow through with your existing clients after the sale or service is rendered, you are missing out on word-of-mouth advertising that is the gold of your marketing efforts.

When a friend tells you what great service or product she has received from a company, do you take notice? Sure you do. However, if some company were to claim that same great service or product in a paid advertisement, would you find that as credible as the testimonial from your friend? Which of the two would cause you to try that company? Your friend's comments, of course! Why? You trust her opinion. This is the power of word-of-mouth advertising.

How do you get your existing clients motivated to become your loudest, best cheerleaders?

You institute a referral program. If you do not have one, you need to think about creating one. If you have one, is it working? Does it propel existing customers into action? Maybe it is time to refresh it. Look at it from your client's perspective. What perk or bonus can you offer that will move the client into taking action and making the referral? Here are some ideas. You can offer:

- Free products or services

- Discounts on future products or services

- Monetary awards or gift cards

- Upgraded shipping

- Priority scheduling

- Exclusive status

- Invitation-only events

Must you have a referral program? Of course not! Most clients may already tell their friends when they receive truly exceptional service. Having a program, can motivate others to make that referral!

How do you propel your business practices over the top into truly exceptional service for your clients? It is what you do *after* the sale that makes a difference. If you do not check with your clients and show them you care about their happiness with your product and service, how likely are you to receive repeat business or referrals? This is what's in it for YOU as an entrepreneur.

- Are you sending clients a survey and asking for feedback, suggestions, product and service ideas?

- Are you sending clients a personal handwritten note of thanks? Even if you have to use a service or hire someone with good handwriting to send it?

- Are you adding each client to your calendar for follow through? For example, a hair stylist knows her client will be due for a cut in six weeks. She could schedule a reminder at five weeks, or better yet, provide *priority scheduling* and offer to schedule the next appointment before the client leaves.

- Do you have a product-based business? Follow through with a phone call and ask if the customer is happy with your product. They might not have time to call you. It is very important to not solicit the next sale in this call. You are calling to make sure the customer is happy. If you are afraid of the phone, it may be because you are asking for the sale instead of making the call about the customer. What if the customer is not happy with the product? It is not the right color, right size, right smell. If that does happen, apologize and be honest. Ask, how can you make this right? Be willing to compromise and know what you can give in these situations.

- What if too much time has passed since the purchase? It is never too late to follow through. Your phone call may sound like this, "Sally, I was just thinking of you! I know you bought product XYZ, and I was wondering how that worked out for you."

Do not just call after a sale. Call for other reasons, such as:

- Ask for a testimonial to use on your website.

- Invite them to an upcoming event.

- Ask if they want to connect on social networking sites, such as Facebook® and if they would "Like" your fan page.

- Ask for their birth date for the birthday club you are going to start.

Be purposeful in creating opportunities for re-connecting in ways that develop your relationships with your clients and customers.

> *"Consumers are statistics. Customers are people."*
> —Stanley Marcus, American entrepreneur

Business Card Follow Up

What about those business cards from events? How do you follow up with potential new customers?

First, you need a system to make the most of your first meeting and to prevent you from losing those cards!

When you meet someone, do you listen? I mean, really hear what they say and remain completely present, so you can connect?

My best networking tip when you go to an event or conference, especially if you are a little shy and are stepping out of your comfort zone, is to look for people who are sitting or standing alone. If they look shy or uncomfortable, make it your mission to bring them out. They will never forget you for making them feel comfortable.

So, you've engaged in conversation, listened, shared and exchanged information. Do you then go home and wait for the phone ring? It doesn't happen, does it?

Right after the event, write a few notes on the person's card. Note where you met them, the date and a word or two to remind you about who they are. Jot down something you discussed. I keep a fine tip Sharpie® pen in my bag to write on UV-coated cards.

You might want to code your cards based on how warm a potential client the person is. You can:

- Rate them from one to five, with five being the hottest.

- Color code them green, yellow, red, with red being the hottest.

- Fold the corners down—two corners for hottest, one corner for warm, no corner for low priority.

Always put cards in the same place! Maybe it's a certain compartment of your purse or the back side of your business card compartment.

As soon as you get back to your office or home, put the cards in a designated follow-up bin. Get started with following through.

Your Follow-Through Plan

After you have a system to prevent contact loss and to avoid delays in connecting, implement your follow-through plan. It takes at least seven positive connection points before a customer feels loyal to you. In today's fast-paced world, the consumer is driven by convenience and technology. More than seven connections may be needed for that loyalty to be felt.

Do you have a system—a plan you follow every time? No? No worries. I'm giving you mine. My business doubled when I started using this plan. Adopt my plan, then tweak it to fit your business.

If you already have a plan, is it working? Do you have so much business you are turning it away? Are you gaining the maximum benefit from what you are putting in? Read on. You might gain a few, new ideas to try!

Step One: The Quick Email

The day after the event, or that night if it is a daytime event, send a short, simple email to each person. Do not send a group email. Write something like this:

• "It was so nice to have met you at [event]."

• "Glad we had a chance to talk at [event]."

• "I am looking forward to getting to know you better."

Make sure your email signature block includes your contact information, business name and what your company does. To add this to your signature block, answer this question, *how do you improve your client's lives?* Here is my signature—the actual signature is bigger and bolder than this representation.

Elizabeth McCormick
Independent Longberger Branch Leader

Providing beauty and function with quality home decor products

Call me at 469-766-7894
Shop online 24/7 at www.longaberger.com/elizabeth
Friend me on FACEBOOK at www.facebook.com/
elizabethmccormick1999

This email is being sent to you by me, your Independent Longaberger Home Consultant. If you prefer not to receive future email updates from me, please reply to this email and type "unsubscribe" in the subject line. My business address is . . . .

Send me an email, and you will see it when I respond!

Step Two: Get Social

After the email is sent, either at the same sitting or within two days, search for that potential new client on Facebook, LinkedIn®, Twitter® and whatever other social media you are on. Make a request to connect with them. Be sure to add a personal comment in the request, such as, "So happy we met at [event]. Looking forward to connecting."

Step Three: Put Pen to Paper

Within the next week, write a handwritten note. Use branded

stationery if you have it. If not, a thank-you note will work. I have gained more new business from this step than any other. Customers call me as soon as they receive the note. It is worth its weight in gold!

When was the last time you received a personal handwritten, snail mail, paper note? What do you open first in your mail? Maybe a check first, I'll give you that, and then the handwritten note is a close second.

Again, your message is simple and similar to the quick email. Thank them for their time and for reconnecting. If you talked about something specific, be sure to mention this in the note, too. Include a business card, so they have your contact information.

So, what happens when an event is larger, and there are many leads to follow through? Categorize your contacts, separate your *hot* leads from the warm and cool and prioritize them. It may take longer to complete your follow-through with the cooler leads. The key is to follow through!

When you mail the note, add a task to your calendar to call each potential new client in three to five days, depending on your mail service. You want enough time for them to have received their card and not so much time that it is awkward.

Step Four: Pick up the Phone

When the date you marked comes up on your calendar, contact your potential client by phone. They will have recently received your card and will remember you. This is a *warm* call.

Say something like, "I'm calling to thank you for taking your time to talk with me at [event]."

Then state your purpose for the call, again *not* asking for a sale! Here are some ideas:

- Invite him or her to upcoming events.

- Ask him or her to attend a future networking meeting. Encourage the person to come with you to hear a speaker.

- Provide a business referral.

Ask if the person would like to receive your newsletter and what is in it for them—special offers to save money, recipes, business tips that provide value. Thank them again.

Step Five: Create a Value-Packed Newsletter

An email newsletter or snail mail version for current and prospective customers can add value to your business and keep customers connected.

What to put in your newsletter? Include:

- Solutions to your customer's needs

- Your message or story

- Testimonials from happy, satisfied customers

- Product or service uses

- Announcements about new products and services

- Relevant articles (properly credited and linked to their website if not your own)

Never add anyone to your newsletter without permission! Always ask. Just meeting them does not give you permission to send a mass marketing piece. This is called *spam*. The potential damage to your business's reputation or having your company's domain blocked by Internet service providers is not worth it.

Step Six: Invite

Inviting is about creating opportunities for future relationship building. I do five customer appreciation events a year—each with a theme and a charitable aspect tied to the event—to build relationships with existing and potential clients. Whether it is a party, a fundraiser, an after-hours VIP invitation-only event or a networking event, you are creating an opportunity to get to know customers better and for them to get to know you.

Step Seven: Ask Their Opinion

All people have a need to be heard. Whether your prospect has the time to respond or not, they will appreciate that you cared enough to ask their opinion. Send a survey, ask for a vote on the date and time of an event, the food, the entertainment—use anything you can that will give them a choice.

Make it a contest with a prize or get ideas from your customers and create a Facebook contest with the most likes or votes for that idea winning something of value! Give customers an opportunity to get involved in your business and create a strong bond. They will refer customers to you and start promoting your business for you!

Step Eight: Keep at It

It may take a while before someone feels compelled to contact you. Remember how busy we are? Our clients and potential clients are busy, too. You need to keep making connections to keep your business in the front of their minds, so they think of you when they are ready. Here are some additional ideas:

- Periodically send an article from a magazine or newspaper that would interest them.

- Mix up the media—snail mail, email, in-person get-togethers, social media updates and messages, phone calls, surveys, video conferencing and so on.

- Try new things!

Schedule connecting time on your calendar for following through with your customers and potential customers. Make it a priority for your business plan, and you will find that it is time well spent when you see your business grow.

Customize a follow-up plan for your business that best suits the needs of your customers and ensures you follow through. Write it down and post it by your computer. Create a follow-through checklist for each event that contains all of the steps you will follow after the event.

You are investing the money in networking, meetings and conferences. Don't you want to make the most of it? Don't you want to see results? Business growth? Sales? Future business? Remember, the key part of following up is following through—then watch your business grow!

Special *Woman Entrepreneur Extraordinaire* Offer

Go to www.yourinspirationalspeaker.com/WEE and request your free follow-up plan consultation. A $250 value!

ELIZABETH MCCORMICK

Inspirational Speaker, Networking Expert and Business Coach

(469) 766-7894
elizabeth@yourinspirationalspeaker.com
www.yourinspirationalspeaker.com

Elizabeth coaches entrepreneurs on how to improve their marketing reach, social media brand and sales strategies. She is an independent John C. Maxwell® team certified speaker, trainer and coach. The success with her follow-up systems has been proven within her Longaberger® Direct Sales business. As a result of using her systems, Elizabeth has experienced double-digit growth in sales, sponsoring and team development. In 2010, Elizabeth was awarded the prestigious "Spirit of Longaberger" Award, given to one sales consultant in the nation for her willingness to share, care and inspire others. She also earned the "Leadership Distinction 2010" Award for the highest performing team in her team size category. Elizabeth has facilitated training at nine national conventions, including three times as a main-stage arena speaker.

An inspirational speaker, Elizabeth relates the challenges she faced as a female Black Hawk helicopter pilot and warrant officer for the United States Army to everyday obstacles that can be overcome.

Elizabeth believes that positive thinking and persistence coupled with action can break down barriers. She lives in the Dallas, Texas, area with her husband, Keith, daughter, Adara, and son, Luke.

Information Products Equal Accelerated Cash Flow

How to Easily Create Products to Add Visibility, Credibility and Profitability

By Michele Scism

*F*or entrepreneurs, whether you are a service provider or own a retail business, it is important to create a consistent and steady flow of new prospects, clients and cash to maintain your business and your sanity. Information products are a quick and easy way to attract new prospects, become known as a leading authority in your industry and differentiate yourself from your competitors. That's why, over the next few pages, I am going to show you how to quickly and easily create information products for any industry, improve your financial success from where you find yourself right now and have someone else do most of the work for you.

Yes, Virginia, Information Products Do Work for All Industries

As a business strategist, I work with business owners in a wide variety of businesses. One of the questions I often hear is, "How could this work for me?" I might be talking with someone in the trucking industry, an attorney, a dentist, an owner of a gardening center, a dancer—the list goes on and on. My answer to each of them and to you is simple. You have information that someone else wants to know. That is exactly what an informational product is.

I have a friend who is a retired Marine fighter pilot, and he sells a very successful information product called *The Fighter Pilot Power Pack.* We all have information that others would pay to know. Do you hear the words "How did you do that?" from others about something you do? Are your colleagues or clients asking you questions about something you could turn into an information product?

Information Products Can Take a Variety of Forms

Wikipedia defines information products as *"any final product in the form of information that a person needs to have."* That seems somewhat vague to me, and I love that it is vague because I get to make it whatever I want it to be. You do not have to do what all of your colleagues are doing. Take a risk and do not just think outside the box—dance and sing your way to the bank outside the box.

One of the reasons I find this really easy and fun is the fact that people like to learn in different ways. That means you can develop your information products by putting together different formats of learning. You could include an audio portion with a written portion or even include an interactive format. Let's take a look at different forms of information products.

Books and ebooks. An easy and inexpensive format to transfer the knowledge you have to others is by writing a book. When I wrote my first book, *Makeover Your Business in 6 Weeks or Less* in early 2010, it was the culmination of a dream. I had been saying for at least five years that I was going to write a book. However, I had no clue where to start, and I thought it was going to be a daunting task. Guess what I found out? A book does not have to be a novel to be a successful tool for business owners. My book is only 88 pages long, self-published and has helped me gain leading authority status in my industry. By the way, this book is my fourth book. What could you write about?

Audios. Don't you just love audio? You can pop a CD in your car and listen while you are driving or download an mp3 or podcast to your iPod® and be learning while you are working out. Do not discount the power of audio when you are creating your information products. We live in a very mobile society, and the more mobile you make your information, the more valuable you are to your audience.

Videos. I think the use of video as an informational product and a marketing tool is extremely underused by business owners. Did you know that according to YouTube®, people watch more than 33,000,000 videos per hour on their website alone? I think this is proof that people love video and that it can be a powerful tool in your information product arsenal.

Workbooks and binders. Whether it is a three-ring binder or a spiral workbook, your clients will feel like they are getting more value for their money when you include either of these in your information product.

Templates, spreadsheets and charts. Would you like an easy way to add value to an information product? Create a template or spreadsheet that relates to the information you are selling. They will make your audience feel like you are going the extra mile to make their lives easier. For example, I once purchased an information product that was focused on how to create tele-seminars. As a bonus, we received a checklist to help us remember the steps for creating a successful tele-seminar.

Online membership sites. Another favorite of mine is to add online information that only the purchaser can get to. It is easy to develop a basic web page that is password protected, so only the purchaser has access to it.

Make More with Your Information Products

Now that you have an idea of what pieces could be included in an information product, let's look at how you can turn a $12 book into a $97 informational product.

Let's say you wrote a book about gardening. What could you do? You could:

- Turn it into an ebook that could be delivered electronically.

- Record a series of three- to five-minute videos that show you using certain gardening tools. Four or five of these videos would be fabulous. Think of other topics you could cover in videos.

- Create a chart that shows people what time of the year to plant certain plants.

- Create a private Facebook® group. Only those who purchase the package can become members of the group, giving them the ability to speak to other would-be gardeners about gardening issues.

- Add three mp3 recordings of you interviewing the world's leading gardening experts. You could interview an expert on roses, on soil and on organic gardening. By the way, since I am definitely not a gardener, I got these ideas by researching Google® to see what people were looking for in the gardening arena!

So what do you have now?

- An ebook

- Five videos on gardening tools

- A planting chart

- An invitation to join a private Facebook group

- Three expert interviews that are downloadable mp3s

This entire package of products can be delivered through email, so the only cost you have is the cost to create the content the first time. Is that $12 book now worth $97? If you are a gardener who thinks you need this information, you bet it is.

Information Product Development in Four Quick, Easy Steps

I hope at this point you are excited about the possibilities of including information products in your business's product funnel. However, before you start creating, you first must do a little planning. The following sequence can help you have your product developed in the next week to ten days.

Step One: Figure Out Your Subject and Your Audience

Begin by answering a few questions:

- What do you know that others are always asking you to help them with? Look specifically at things you take for granted. For example, if you are a successful real estate investor, you could teach others how to buy and sell real estate for a profit.

- Gather information on what your target market wants, so you can be sure what you are offering is something they are looking for. What are the hot topics in your industry? What types of products are people already purchasing?

- What have you created that can be repurposed? Maybe you have a blog, and you could put several of your blog posts together to create an ebook.

Step Two: Decide on the Price Point for Your Product

You do not have to decide on the exact price at this point. Just choose a range. Maybe this product is going to be in the $45 to $97 range.

Maybe you are looking for a product in the $100 to $200 range.

Notice, you are setting this range *before* defining what is included in your information product. I find that if I know what price range I am shooting for, it is easier for me to determine how many and what size pieces I need to include. To determine this range, you might want to do some research about what others in your industry are doing and what your potential clients are already paying.

Step Three: Decide on the Pieces of Your Information Product

I wrote earlier about the gardening book that turned into a $97 information product. In this step, you want to think through what you could do in your price range. Do not forget about what you might already have developed that you could repurpose.

If you are creating an ebook, do you have pre-written material you can use? If it is going to be an audio-and-transcript program, have you already recorded a call that can be transcribed, or do you need to schedule a free tele-seminar? If it is going to be a bigger home-study course, do you have the material already, or do you need to get in front of a live audience and record it?

Here is an example. I once recorded a tele-seminar about how I added 1,000 fans to my Facebook fan page in thirty days. I had so many people register for that call, I did it twice. After the success of the call, I started to think this might make a fantastic information product. I sent the audio recording to my transcriptionist, who charged me $60 to transcribe the call and turn it into a word document. I hired a graphic designer to create a product image and cover for my new word document and paid him about $75. I hired a website designer to put together an online sales page using Wordpress®, so I could market the product, which cost me about $250. By the way, this is one of the ways you get others to do all the work for you. The only part I actually did was record the one-hour call.

My total cost for developing this product was $385 plus my time for recording the call. I call it *How I Grew My Facebook Fan Page from 1 to 1026 Fans in 30 Days* and sell it for $27. At this price point, the fifteenth sale covered all of my expenses. In the first six months, I sold 100 copies, so my one hour of work paid me $2,315. Since all of it is digital and automated, I do absolutely nothing and watch the money be deposited into my checking account. This is my favorite part! If you would like to see a sample sales page that I used to sell this information product you can see it at www.YourFanPageSuccess.com.

The fabulous thing is this: I can continue to sell this product for a very long time. If I can sell ten copies a week at $27, I have an annual increase in my cash flow of $14,040. Not bad for a product I do not even have to touch.

It is important to note that if I wanted to turn this into a physical product, it simply means creating a CD of the audio and a workbook from the transcript, which I could probably have produced and shipped for less than $10 using a fulfillment company. At that point, I would probably increase the price of the package to $37 to cover this cost.

Think about the $97 gardening product from earlier. Selling just ten of those per week would mean an annual increase in your cash flow of $50,440 (520 buyers x $97). For many business owners, this would double or triple their cash flow. One of the interesting things about information products is that they are relationship builders. If you can get 25 percent of those who purchase your gardening information product to purchase your next product, which is priced at $497, you would add an additional $64,610 to your cash flow (520 buyers x 25% = 130 buyers x $497).

Step Four: Create Your Product and Launch It

Now, you have decided on a topic and a market. You know the price and pieces of your product. Only two things remain: Create it and sell it!

First, what do you need to do to create the pieces? Do you need to hire a transcriber, a graphic person, a web designer or someone to write sales copy for you? Do you have the right tools to create the pieces you are going to create yourself?

Get out there and take action. It is time to put the plan in motion and develop the product.

You also must develop a marketing strategy to sell it! You want to make money from this product. If you do not start telling people about it, you will quickly start to realize it is the best-kept secret in town. I have a product development and launch checklist I use that might give you a little direction.

Checklist for a Successful Product Launch

• Decide on the product.

• Set a launch date.

• How will you sell the product? (tele-seminars, sales page, up-sell)

• Create your launch promotional sequence.

• Start working on developing your product.

• Create value-added free bonuses.

• Build an affiliate program for promotion.

• Write five to twenty articles and blog posts about your subject.

• Have a graphic designer develop your product and website graphics.

- Build your website and back-end pages.

- Be sure you have an online merchant account.

- Create your social networking marketing strategy.

- Test your entire sales process, then test it again and again.

- Launch!

> *"Some people dream of success . . . while others work hard at it."*
> —Author Unknown

With the checklist above and your newfound knowledge about how to easily create profitable information products, it is now time for a decision on your part. You can look at this, make a decision that it is too much work and choose to do nothing. On the other hand, you can choose to take action, start creating your product right away and within a matter of weeks, you could be making money selling your first information product. I hope that you choose the latter since it leads to success!

Special *Woman Entrepreneur Extraordinaire* Offer

Now that you have a plan to create information products, learn how to use Facebook® and LinkedIn® to promote them!

To say "Thank you" for reading my chapter, I would like to give you a 50-percent discount on my virtual Facebook and LinkedIn training program. Visit www.TakeActionGetProfitsVirtual.com and type in coupon code WEE50.

MICHELE SCISM
Decisive Minds™, LLC
Global Social Media Managers
Association™

Rapid Results . . . Strategically

michele@decisiveminds.com
www.decisiveminds.com

Michele Scism is a leading authority on social media and online marketing and the founder of DecisiveMinds.com and the Global Social Media Managers Association™. Her clients call her "The Results Lady" because she is a business strategist who uses her signature "Take Action Get Profits" system to help business owners get visibility and new, loyal clients.

The key to any successful business is visibility and client attraction, and Michele's systems, strategies and business tips focus on that. Her knowledge of and expertise in online marketing and social media marketing have been recognized on several web video shows. She has been interviewed on social media topics, such as Facebook and LinkedIn for business by Kristi Frank, a former contestant on Donald Trump's *The Apprentice® Season 1*, several talk radio shows and many tele-classes.

Michele has a degree in accounting and spent most of her life building her family's trucking business, which she sold in 2007. In January of 2010, she created Decisive Minds with the intention of using her business strategy knowledge to help entrepreneurs get the word out about their business, find new clients and create consistent profits.

Expand Your Business
with an Effective Virtual Team
By Dortha Hise

*C*heck all the statements that apply to you:

- You want help attaining your dreams more efficiently and with more ease.

- You cannot find enough hours in the day to do what needs to be done.

- You are a stay-at-home mom with a side business and are on a constant guilt trip over not being able to balance work and life.

- You need more income and do not have more hours left in the day to earn it.

- You are a *multi-preneur* with several businesses and cannot juggle them all.

- You are frustrated with not having time to do more follow up and track existing clients in a tidy database.

- You are unable to update regularly your social media sites, website and blog.

- Snail mail and email are piling up and phone calls are unreturned.

- You feel like a *zombie-preneur*—walking around mindlessly and aimlessly without direct purpose!

If any—or most—of these statements sound like you, you have reached the point in your business when you need a virtual team to help you get everything done. Your team may consist of one or more persons who can do all of the above for you—and more! Your team can:

- Update your website and related web collateral.

- Do your bookkeeping and invoicing.

- Manage your marketing and public relations.

- Edit and write your materials.

- Manage your contacts and calendar.

- Take on anything you do not have the time or skill to do!

Use the Power of Delegation to Get Things Done

"The first rule of management is delegation. Don't try and do everything yourself because you can't."
—Anthea Turner, English television presenter

Now is the time to delegate. Delegation allows you to multiply your efforts while decreasing your stress. It is fabulous when you can delegate tasks to your own virtual team. You gain their knowledge, expertise and support and get rid of tasks that do not bring you joy, satisfaction or income. This allows you more time for activities that only you can do.

As one client shared with me, "It finally hit me. If I keep going the way I had been—doing everything—I was fracturing my efforts and not really gaining ground in any area. With a team, I can hit all areas and be strong and prosperous."

Why spend your time mailing your own e-newsletter when you could be using that time to book paying business? Move your business to the next level by focusing on what you do well and what you need to do. Avoid burnout, grow your business and reach your dreams with the help of your team.

Let me share with you the eleven key steps to set yourself up for success and build a virtual dream team.

Step One: Choose the Tasks You Can Delegate

This may likely change over time, so you need to revisit this every three months.

What tasks can you delegate to someone else? Choose tasks that require skills you do not have or are not strong in or tasks that take you away from income-producing activities only you can perform. Let's say you are a business coach, and your to-do list includes: find speaking engagements, write a book, create a website, make cold calls and schedule coaching sessions with your clients. Here is an easy way to consider what things you can delegate to a virtual team member. Ask yourself which of these things are tasks only *you* can do?

My experience has shown that coaching sessions with clients cannot be handed off to someone else. Everything else can come off your to-do list and be given to your virtual team!

Step Two: How to Find Team Members

Before you begin your virtual team search, be sure you are clear on what work you need completed and how many hours per week you anticipate these projects will take to complete. For example, you might want an administrative assistant to handle *ad hoc* duties for five hours a week.

Sometimes, the best place to start your research is to ask your colleagues and friends if they use virtual help, what they use their team members for, and where they found their team members.

If no one you know uses a virtual team, here are some resources you can explore. Start with a Google® search for "virtual assistant," "personal assistant" or "virtual assistant directories." You can also attend networking mixers with local businesses or local chambers of commerce where virtual assistants might attend, or you can meet business owners who may utilize the services of virtual assistants. You can also check out organizations that certify virtual assistants, such as Assistu at www.assistu.com or International Virtual Assistants Association at www.ivaa.org.

When you interview potential team members, be sure to ask about the following:

• What is their time zone?

• What are their office hours?

• What is the typical turnaround time on projects?

• What is the hourly rate?

• Is there a "rush rate"?

• Do they require a retainer?

• Is there a discount for retaining them for more hours per month?

• Do they offer packages for their services?

• Do hours roll over from month to month?

• What is the minimum charge per task?

• How do they bill and how often do they bill?

• What is the preferred method of communication—email, phone, interactive web presentation like GoToMeeting™ and so on?

Also, ask them to describe past projects they have worked on that might be similar to yours and have them provide references.

Step Three: Prepare to Delegate

After you have a list of what you want to delegate and have chosen your virtual team members, start to evaluate their characteristics and personalities so you know what you can delegate to each.

This part of the process can be very difficult for some, especially if you are used to doing everything yourself. I recommend starting a sheet for each member of your team to keep track of them in one place. For example, you could list the assignment and to whom it was given, describe the task, identify the criteria for a successful assignment and include a timeline.

Step Four: Describe the Terms of the Project and Expected Outcomes

This is the place to discuss costs, negotiate the scope and terms of the project, set deadlines and so on. This is also where the team member will learn about your business.

There is a learning curve for each new person coming into your team while he or she learns about you, your work style and your business. Typically, a few hours of training time is needed. If you have a very complex business model or have a unique and specific business, your virtual team members may have to spend more time in that learning curve.

Step Five: Keep It Legal

Put in place any contracts, non-disclosure agreements and other legal paperwork, as necessary. If you do not have an attorney on staff to assist you in drafting these documents, there are several resources freely available on the Internet to download. (See also "The Ten Commandments of Small Business Success" by Nancy Lewellen on page 61.)

Step Six: Set a Trial Period or Assignment

Consider the first project as a trial period to ensure that you and your team are working well together. For example, if a virtual assistant is creating your new website and gives you an estimate of ten hours of time, create a checkpoint at a two- to three-hour point to monitor progress, answer questions and develop a plan of attack to move forward.

At the end of the trial period, you will either hire that person to work long-term with you on your team or terminate the relationship if it did not work out. Provide constructive feedback to the person about why it did not work out. This is helpful for both you and the virtual assistant as it will open a dialogue about the project and how both parties felt about it—a forum to discuss what did and did not work. Remember to be constructive since this is not designed to beat up the other person.

Dale Carnegie, an American writer, lecturer and developer of self-improvement courses, suggests that when providing constructive criticism to yourself or to others, dole out a "compliment sandwich." That is, do not focus solely on the negative aspects of a mistake. According to the Dale Carnegie Way® online, "Leave yourself feeling better by ending with a positive outlook and a new way to approach a similar situation." I think of it as stating things that a person has done well, followed by the constructive criticism and ended with another compliment.

"All good criticism should be judged the way art is. You shouldn't read it the way you read history or science."
—Leslie Fielder, Jewish-American literary critic

Step Seven: Establish a Well-Defined Timeline with Goals and Intentions

For example, if you need a project finished by the end of the month, give your team member a week to ten days before that deadline for any changes or edits that may be necessary in the course of the back-and-forth with your team. Be careful not to micromanage all aspects of the project you have just delegated. Trust that the person you have hired is going to address all aspects of the project and come to you with any questions or for any clarification.

Step Eight: Collaborate with Your Team

Work with your team to figure out how many hours each person will spend on his or her respective tasks. I recommend using an online collaboration workflow tool that will allow multiple users to access it, add to it and cross items off it. There are several sites available for free and for fee. Some of these sites are:

- Google documents provides an easy format for creating documents, spreadsheets and other items to keep track of projects and share them with your team.

- TeamWorkLive.com™ allows you to track tasks, centralize communications and share documents and files as well as collaborate with your clients and team.

- Businessitonline.com™ creates a centralized cash flow, documents and calendars for a team.

- Colligo.com allows you to work on projects offline and sync when you are online.

- RemembertheMilk.com™ helps you manage your tasks so you never forget anything.

- WorkFlowy.com helps get everything onto one piece of paper and allows organization of large projects, note taking, journaling and much more.

This creates transparency, so everyone knows what everyone else is doing and how it all fits together.

Step Nine: Establish the Method of Preferred Communication

You want to monitor progress and set team conference calls or emails. When interacting with your team, there must be communication by and among team members that allows everyone to easily translate complex, possibly technical things, into simple, easy-to-understand steps.

This is especially important if you are in a very specific industry with which your team may not be familiar. I have worked with a variety of industries from image consultants to mortgage professionals to business coaches who cater to the financial sustainability of their clients. It is critical to be able to convey the important things about your business without overwhelming your team. The language that is used in your business and industry may be second nature to you, but your team does not necessarily have the same background in what it is that you do.

Step Ten: Establish Payment Policies

Figure out billing frequency and how invoices are to be sent and payment is to be accepted. Some clients I have worked with prefer to be billed monthly while others would like a project-by-project accounting and pay accordingly. If you have provided a retainer for a virtual assistant's services, ensure that you will receive a monthly accounting for those services. There are a variety of ways that you can pay your virtual team, including check, PayPal®, credit card, and others—so be sure to connect with your team and determine what is the preferred method and frequency for billing.

Step Eleven: Use Your Time to Build Your Business

Now that you have a virtual team in place, and you have freed up your time, what will you do to fill that time? Make more money, add more clients, develop new products for your online store? What projects or clients do you need to put some attention on? Your virtual team will give you the time you need to work on your business.

Everyone has the same 24 hours in a day. Hiring a virtual team can help you maximize how you use those hours and help you be more profitable, sustainable and productive in your business.

Your Virtual Team ROI

Like many entrepreneurs, you are probably asking how you can afford to bring someone on and pay him or her. Remember, hiring team members will give you more billable time and bring in more revenue. This revenue will be more than the cost of your team, so you come out ahead. For example, writer and editor Patricia Haddock uses a virtual assistant to help her prepare the PowerPoint® presentations and handouts she uses for her training programs while she does work for her clients. The cost of her assistant is far outweighed by the fees she earns from her clients.

How can you determine the return on investment? One of my clients recently shared that since working with me and other team members, her income stream has grown at least 500 percent. She said that this happened because she has time to complete more projects, find more clients and focus on income-producing activities. For this client, hiring a virtual team has freed her to do the things that only she can do and that are income producing for her business.

Peace of mind and less stress are also benefits of having a virtual team. If you know you can send something to your team in the middle of the night, and it will be done by mid-morning the next day, you have peace of mind. Having a strong support system in place always means someone says, "Yes" to your projects and is ready to be in action to support you.

Go back to the beginning of this chapter. If any of those statements fit you, it is time to build a virtual team. Consider using a virtual assistant who can take over the administrative tasks you currently handle. Find a writer or editor who can help you prepare clear, compelling client materials. Hire an accountant or bookkeeper to take over billing. Start now to expand your business with an effective virtual team.

Special *Woman Entrepreneur Extraordinaire* Offer

Is your website drawing the potential customers and clients you want to attract? Is your blog current and market-driven? Contact me at dortha@dorthahise.com or (916) 817-6878 for a free evaluation and find out how you can reach customers and clients more effectively. Remember, the brand is you!

DORTHA HISE

Your success is my business!

(916) 817-6878
dortha@dorthahise.com
www.dorthahise.com

Dortha Hise is passionate about helping others be successful. Born and raised in California, she began her first business at the age of 11, breeding hamsters and selling the offspring to local pet stores. She graduated from Loyola University of Chicago with a bachelor of arts in psychology in 1998 and received a bachelor of science in criminal justice in 2003 from University of Nevada, Las Vegas.

A serial entrepreneur, Dortha runs a successful virtual consulting business and a web design and development business. She also serves as a leadership representative with Avon® products. She offers a variety of support to her clients from research and phone calls to web design and social media support.

An ardent advocate for breast cancer cure, Dortha has walked in the Sacramento American Cancer Society Making Strides® walk since 2006. In 2010, after losing a close friend to breast cancer, Dortha raised more than $2,000 and walked forty miles in the Avon Walk for Breast Cancer®. Dortha and her best friend and husband, Jason, have coordinated medical screening clinics to benefit the Shriners Hospital for Children® and currently oversee screening clinics in 23 counties in northern California.

Quick Tips to Put Your Website to Work

By Tammy Tribble

*M*arketing is the act of telling everyone about your amazing business. Internet marketing is doing it on the web. That means having a website that establishes you as an expert in your field, captures user information to stay in contact through email and drives traffic to your site. Your goal is to connect your target market with your incredible products or services.

Whether you are getting a new website or have an existing one, the same questions and considerations apply.

- What is the main goal of your site?
- What are your three highest priorities? Is it to sell a product or service? Create credibility for your business? Attract new clients? Establish yourself as an expert? Get booked as a speaker? Increase your list of potential clients?
- How can you make your website work for you?

Your business is amazing, and you have so much to offer. Let's explore marketing-savvy tips that will put your website to work as you grow your business with ease.

Tip One: Be True to Your Identity

All business communications start with the brand. The technical definition of branding is the identity of a specific product, service or business. It can be a name, sign, symbol, color, slogan or even sound. The reality is that branding is so much more—it is the emotional feeling a client associates with your mark.

This emotion is based on a promise being delivered and an expectation of consistent value and worth. The client feels comfortable when purchasing a product or service from a familiar brand. It is this emotional connection to the client that is the foundation of your growing business and the launching point for building a brand identity and standing out from the crowd.

Branding also benefits your business by adding value. Businesses with a strong brand and professional website can charge more for products and services than a competitor with an identical product or service that is not professionally branded.

Having a strong brand legitimizes businesses and allows competition with more established companies. A professional website makes businesses look more credible, established and bigger. Also, branded businesses are typically more resilient in troubled economic times. (See "Communicating Your Personal Brand" by Melanie Fitzpatrick on page 107.)

Think of your website as a major component of your brand identity. People expect a business to have a website. When it is consistent with your brand, it establishes your identity and helps you become more recognizable to clients as a professional business. To learn more about business branding and identity, see my chapter in *Mom Entrepreneur Extraordinaire,* published by Thrive Publishing™ in 2010 at www.mimeticdesigns.com.

Tip Two: Make Obvious What You Do

Not only do you have to make it obvious *what* you do, you also have to do it *quickly*. The average user takes less than *one second* to form an opinion about your business from your site. You only have *four seconds* to communicate exactly what you do and for whom you do it before they leave your site and go elsewhere.

On your customer-focused site, it helps to draw attention to your professional services by highlighting each product or service and making it obvious what your business offers. Present key offerings with informational text, images and links for easy navigation and customer sales.

Tip Three: Keep It Simple

Make it easy for the user to get the product or service they want and make sure that important information is "above the fold." This is the area higher on the page and does not require scrolling down to see the content.

Start with a clear navigation that runs horizontally on the page. Keep the main navigation items to seven or less and utilize drop-down menus for sub-pages. If you have several products or services, highlight them all in one place as topics, so your clients can choose to view a specific highlighted topic on its own page on your website. Feature these with titles and images on the main page or in the sidebar for easy access. Think of your site as a house, with several places you want the visitor to go. By having several ways to get to the same page, you make it simple for the user and increase the likelihood of an interaction.

The important items should never be more than two clicks away or you may lose some potential clients. Also, it is great to have a main services page, but keep your individual services on separate pages to give each the attention it deserves. This will allow your clients to be directed easier to the service they are most interested in and to see it at its best.

Tip Four: Convert Users to Potential Clients and Build Your List

One of the main goals of most sites is to increase your list of potential clients. This allows you to keep in front of these potential clients with information, e-zines, news and special offerings through email, also known as email marketing campaigns.

Use your website to collect email addresses by providing a compelling offer that entices users to subscribe to your email list and collect your free offer. Your offer not only acts as an incentive to capture user information, but it also establishes you as an expert and increases your credibility. Use this offer to highlight services you provide and be sure to include your contact information.

As your email list grows, you may want to exchange lists with complementary businesses that have the same ideals and values as yours. This is a win-win partnership in which all participants agree to share their contacts. You email their offer to your list and you get to put your offer in front of a whole new group of potential clients.

Tip Five: Be Social

Interaction makes for a dynamic and lively environment that allows users to help promote your website and services while helping you in your search engine rankings.

By connecting with your clients on social networks like Twitter®, Facebook®, LinkedIn® and others, you can educate your clients about your business, tell them how to get in touch with you and create links back to your website. This is also a chance to continue to showcase you as an expert by posting valuable information and special offers. You can also ask your social networks to "like" your site by attaching code provided by the social network. This code places a button on the site that allows the user to "like" it. On some social networks, there are also options to "share" your site, or blog with their contacts or direct them to your fan page.

Blogging is a great venue for interaction and another way to show your expertise. The longer you keep a user on your site, the more opportunity you have to convert them to a client. A content-rich blog is a great way to keep them coming back. Having a blog and posting to it on a regular basis adds new content to your site and is very helpful for getting found on the Internet. Search engines have programs called "spiders" that search sites, compile keywords and rank them according to content on their search engine. New content is like food for the spiders, and it adds to your search engine rankings.

Another good idea is to be a guest blogger on other websites and have links back to yours in the content you provide. There are lots of different blog sites, called "directories," that allow you to register your blog and link back to your site. You can also post a small part of your blog content on all your social networks and direct the user back to your site for the full content.

Tip Six: Show Clients You Know Your Stuff

Show credentials, association logos and frequently asked questions (FAQ) pages to help your clients understand more about your business and establish credibility. Place these logos prominently on the home page and make sure there is a navigation button to the FAQ page of your site.

If you are featured in publications like magazines or books, make sure they show up on the home page. Print publications are golden for establishing trust and credibility, and—if you are a speaker—help you stand out from others by giving you additional opportunities to get in front of more potential clients.

Include videos, podcasts, articles, e-books and blog posts—anything that you have to share with your clients—to keep them up to date with more access to information about you and your business. Keeping current and providing a content-rich website adds value and keeps your clients coming back.

Tip Seven: Show Off a Bit

Proudly display a client list on your website, include testimonials and list publications to solidify your credibility as an expert in your field and to show off the great things people have said about you and your business.

Testimonials are the most effective and inexpensive way to establish trust with a potential client. The most visited pages on a website by the average user interested in your product or service are the testimonials page and FAQ pages. Sprinkle testimonials throughout the site, as well as on a page of their own. As far as credibility, the video testimonial is highest, the testimonial with picture is next, and the testimonial with text is last. With video on phones and camera, along with YouTube®, it has never been easier to add video testimonials to your site.

Tip Eight: Be Accessible

Make it easy for your clients to contact you by listing your phone number and email address in an easy-to-find location. Adding it on multiple pages, or even every page—especially the front page—will help your clients reach you with ease. If you are a local business, feature your address prominently and create a free listing for your business on the numerous local business sites. Both Google® and Yahoo® have these listings, along with many others.

On your "Contact Us" page, add a map to your location. There is also the option of adding a form to this page that the user has to fill out in order to contact you. If you decide to use a form, make it short and simple because the more steps the user has to take, the less likely they are to contact you.

Tip Nine: Be Clear and Compelling

Your content should be easily accessible to all users, customer-focused and benefit-driven. Use small words, short sentences and brief paragraphs and keep the style conversational. Make it easy to skim for content, using headlines, subheads and bullets to communicate the main points.

In your content, especially the headlines and subheads, use key words that the user will enter to find your site. Search engines look for key words in these areas first, then in the body copy and then in the descriptions you attach to images.

Video and audio tell the story and give the user an opportunity to connect in a way that text does not allow. Pictures are worth a thousand words and make the site interesting to view.

Tip Ten: Ask for the Business

Sell the benefits on your site, not just the features of what you have to offer. A person who signs up for a diet program does so because they see the benefit of having a lean, healthy body, not because they get shakes or pre-packaged meals. The same applies to your products and services. What are the benefits to the user? Have you communicated these in the key messages and backed it up in heads, subheads and body copy?

Now, ask for the business and include a clear call to action on every service or product you offer. Make sure you have a compelling offer with the email capture box and ask clearly for the user to "sign up now" or "register now."

When you describe a service on that page of your site, have a clear call to action in the text. Add "Read more" or "Click here to order" on every service you provide and make sure your products all have a "Buy now" button. Make it easy for people to purchase by accepting credit and debit cards. Place those icons on your site so the user knows immediately what cards you accept.

On your business cards, include a call to action. Have text on your cards that direct the user to your site to sign up for your compelling offer. When you are networking, include your call to action when you talk about your business. After your benefit, customer-focused elevator speech, ask them to come to your site and sign up for your amazing, incredible offer.

Be Focused, Flexible and Have Fun

Developing a marketing-savvy site takes focused energy and the ability to be flexible while having fun. A content-rich site with interaction and current content takes commitment and time. By focusing on your website at least thirty minutes a few times a week, you will build a site that attracts the clients you want and is a valuable resource users enjoy visiting again and again.

Stay flexible and adaptable. Once you have your compelling offer, send it to people in your target market and get their feedback. It may be that what you thought was valuable is not what your users want. Be willing to adapt the content to the users' needs and wants and continue to get feedback to create a more customer-focused site.

Monitor your blog to determine which posts get the most attention and add similar content that attracts your potential clients. Be willing to use this information to continue to grow and evolve your business in a natural and organic way.

Have fun with the process and enjoy the journey. It began with you putting your heart and soul into your business. You were excited to help others and thrilled that your passion could be your livelihood. Keep that energy and joy as you continue to grow your business and develop your website.

Start now! Make a commitment today to apply at least one of these ten tips to your current site. If your presence on the web no longer serves your business or you are getting a site for the first time, call a web professional to help you develop a marketing-savvy site that works for you and communicates your amazing business clearly and succinctly. It is so exciting to see a vision for a business become a reality!

Special *Woman Entrepreneur Extraordinaire* Offer

Is your website working for you? Mimetic Design is happy to offer a free website evaluation to the readers of *Woman Entrepreneur Extraordinaire*. This $97 value includes a comprehensive questionnaire and one-hour evaluation. Contact me for your free evaluation.

TAMMY TRIBBLE
Mimetic Design Systems, Inc.

Making the vision a reality

510-881-8446
tammyt@mimeticdesigns.com
www.mimeticdesigns.com

Tammy Tribble is founder and creative director of Mimetic Systems, Inc. She graduated with honors from California College of the Arts with a bachelor of fine arts in graphic design and has been self-employed for more than ten years. After her daughter was born in 2004, she became an official *mompreneur.*

For Tammy, being a graphic designer is so much more than designing a logo, brochure or website. It is about helping her clients fulfill their dreams! As a member of their success team, Tammy asks pertinent questions that clearly define her client's short- and long-term goals. She makes suggestions, provides input and often writes the copy for her clients. She is totally committed to her client's satisfaction and will do what it takes to make sure the project meets or exceeds expectations. She looks at the big picture, helps her clients envision the possibilities and provides the tools to make that vision a reality!

Tammy specializes in the best corporate graphics for emerging and growing businesses all over North America. She has worked with amazing entrepreneurs and mompreneurs, and her business has prospered through referrals and client loyalty.

The Convergence of Marketing, Sales and Public Relations
Navigation for Small Business Success
By LynAnn King

There is no doubt about it, trying to navigate the deep, murky waters of marketing, sales and public relations is akin to setting sail around the world in a dinghy. Very few entrepreneurs embody the brash showmanship and salesmanship of the legendary P.T. Barnum, founder of Ringling Bros. & Barnum & Bailey Circus®. You may not realize it, but just like P.T. Barnum, you've erected a "Big Tent"— an established business under which everything you do converges. Now comes the fun part—embarking on a multi-faceted promotional plan that gets your business recognized and rewarded. That is, unless you allow yourself to be derailed by the fear of marketing yourself. Fortunately, armed with the right marketing, sales, and public relations tools, you will be able to navigate these tumultuous waters with confidence.

Not so long ago, marketing was considered to be the all-encompassing umbrella under which all other promotional disciplines such as advertising, public relations, events and internal and external communications were sheltered. Today, the lines have blurred and seem to be converging, despite their individual specializations. Every business has to embrace marketing, sales and public relations to rise above the competition.

What exactly does that mean? It means that you have to take an outward, extroverted approach and become proficient at selling yourself, your brand, your product offerings and the benefits you provide another person or business. It is an art to become both detailed in your expertise and then promote that value benefit. People buy people. Romancing your prospects through the "sales funnel" to becoming your clients is about being of service, approachable and engageable. Know, like and trust is the new mantra.

Early in my career, I had a grueling computer industry-driven day job in Silicon Valley and moonlighted at night as a jazz singer. When Silicon Valley crashed, I decided to try my luck in dinner theater entertainment in the San Francisco Bay Area, where I found my marketing voice.

Fortunately, over the years I had built a solid organizational reputation with the local chamber of commerce and had founded and launched the Professional Women's Chamber Connection (PWCC) luncheon series that included 12 chambers. I formed a partnership with the Downtown Merchants Association, targeting the affluent downtown community with a large number of upscale restaurants. Together, we launched the Dine Around Passport Program, a multi-faceted, month–long marketing, sales and public relations big-idea promotion.

I was knee-deep in coordinating every essential element of this broad-based promotion from visionary creation through completion. Finally, it all came together like a harmonic convergence. Most significantly, my personal job crisis turned into career confidence with the successful launch of my new business.

This chapter will give you a greater understanding of marketing, sales, and public relations and some tips on how to apply them in your business. By embracing the elements of each of these disciplines, you can be confident in moving forward with your plan of action that gets you known, liked and trusted, resulting in a business you love and clients that are right for you.

Marketing

Selling of products or services: the business activity of presenting products or services in such a way as to make them desirable.

If I could teach one thing about marketing, it would be how to write compelling copy, or content. It has to be written for the reader— your customer. Content often is written from the entrepreneur's perspective. Some examples are, "We are so excited to announce," or "We are celebrating our 20th year." These kinds of communications have nothing to do with the customer. Your content *must* be relevant to the reader. They want to know, "What's in it for *me*?"

Keep the primary focus of the copy on your target customer.

Marketing breaks down into the four Ps:

- **Product.** Something you have that is needed or desired—your specific focus and expertise.
- **Price.** The amount a customer is willing to pay for the product or service.
- **Place.** Location where the product can be purchased, downloaded or viewed. It could be a physical store, an online virtual store or consultation services.
- **Promotion.** All communications a marketer uses in the market-place. It can include advertising, sponsorship, affiliate marketing, publicity, personal selling sales promotion.

In most cases, entrepreneurs are involved in every aspect of the business. You are your business. Let's add two more Ps to the marketing concept: persuasion and passion.

- **Persuasion.** Motivating your potential customers to believe and trust you—to buy from you—not your competition. It's glorious to build that essential trust, first in your abilities and secondly, in your products and services' excellence. Having awesome integrity and commitment to deliver exquisite customer service is an excellent way. Engaging and contributing in social media activities is another fabulous way to attract your new clients.

- **Passion.** Loving what you do. As a publicist, I have both a passion for my profession and my clients. It helps to have a balanced personal life that includes rejuvenation, quality time with those you love and fun activities. Passion cannot be faked. Follow through on a personal aspiration. Take an acting, singing or dancing class. Allow other parts of your personal self to fully express, and it will transcend to your confidence in sales and promotions. If you do not wake up each morning eager to take on whatever the day brings, then you need to figure out what's draining your energy. Reawaken the passion that got you motivated to start a business in the first place.

Sales

Selling of something–the transfer of something to the ownership or use of somebody else, or the provision of something, for example, a service, in exchange for an agreed-upon amount of money.

Almost everyone who has ever been in sales has this timeless book *How to Win Friends and Influence People,* by Dale Carnegie, reissued by Simon & Schuster in 2009. The best salespeople are extremely good listeners and are adept at getting their prospects to talk. By attentive listening and asking the right questions, they learn what their sales prospects need and want right now. They don't push . . . they *pull* information *from* their prospects.

> *"If you can dream it, then you can achieve it. You will get all you want in life if you help enough other people get what they want."*
> —Zig Ziglar, American sales and motivational speaker

This quote speaks to the very heart of how to be successful in sales, despite today's chaotic, uncertain business environment. In Ziglar's motivational sales presentations, he talks frequently about "sharpening the sword." Work with an executive coach to bring out the best entrepreneur you can be. You need to constantly sharpen your skills and incorporate new, contemporary strategies to be competitive. In other words: Listen. Learn. Lead.

Take a look at just a few of today's new and ongoing business busters:

- **Companies are leaner and meaner.** Employee downsizing, fewer resources and time constraints have severely limited a sales person's chances to land a face-to-face meeting and begin to develop a positive, productive business relationship. (See "Think like a CEO" by Alice Hinckley on page 37.)

- **Prospective buyers are immune to the old sales pitches.** The same old sales pitches do not work today. You have to earn trust by engaging with prospects by providing real content and solutions to problems. Business owners are highly informed and want to be heard and taken care of with great follow through. They want to know you care about them. (See "It's Not Stalking...It's Follow Up!" by Elizabeth McCormick on page 143.)

- **Telephone reality.** People are involved, busy, multi-tasking; you may catch them at an inconvenient time. Business leaders are buried in deadlines and deliverables. Today each person has their own preference of being contacted and phone may be their last choice. It could be social media, Email, networking, in-person meetings, personal introductions or by phone. The sales pitch has to break through the chaos. It has to be of value to *them*. Personal introductions, testimonials and connections open the doors for you to walk in with credibility, backed with relationships already in place. (See "Networking and Creating Referral Partners" by Jeanie Breisinger on page 233.)

- **Competition is fierce.** Your product or service may not be unique, so you need to communicate your product or service differential more efficiently and effectively. How *you* communicate how your product or service is different, is what makes the difference. While all this can seem discouraging, remind yourself of this one important fact: You are unique, one of a kind, like no other. So move forward, armed with your special accomplishments and attributes to succeed in the sales game. Be yourself, everyone else is taken! Even my identical twin sister is unique from me.

Public Relations

Promotion of favorable image—the practice or profession of establishing, marketing or employing a favorable relationship between an institution or person and the public.

My definition of publicity is *unpaid, factual or entertaining information supplied to the appropriate media by a publicist or individual on behalf of an organization.*

Here is today's reality check: In our Internet-driven modern world, the traditional public relations practitioner who has not kept up with new media will be lost in cyberspace. The good news for them, and for you, is that even though the principles and practices may have changed, the fundamentals of good publicity presentation remain essential to landing press.

The Elements of a Press Kit

When pitching something to the press, it is customary to start with a personalized pitch letter—to ascertain whether or not this media source is interested in what you are pitching. Here are some essential items of an email press kit that need to be accomplished.

- **An up-to-date media list.** Select the top print newspapers, magazines, radio shows and TV spots that include your target market. Once compiled, it's essential to spend the time calling each source to verify that they are still working at that media distribution, and then to determine whether that reporter or journalist covers the subject matter of your specific business industry. If changed, get the new name and contact info. Also note how they prefer to be contacted. Do a Google® search to learn what that journalist has been writing about—they like that a lot!

- **The email pitch letter.** The subject line has to sizzle. Know the types of articles that journalist prefers and show you are familiar with their specialty. Connecting your story or "your pitch" with current hot topics will get their attention. I had a fertility doctor client around the time of the Octuplets story. My media calls landed us print, radio and TV interviews within days of calling to offer my client for expert commentary. The pitch *must* be timely and capture the imagination of your media target—craft one or two tight paragraphs.

- **The email press release.** A world of caution here: *Never send an email attachment to a journalist unless specifically authorized by that media source.* At the top left of the press release, enter your contact name, phone and email. Next, the headline, which should be intriguing and capture the imagination. Make it provocative and interesting! Don't be boring. For example, *From Reel to Real: AICI Commends the Ad Biz in Their Continuing Trend of Using Real People in Print and Broadcast Campaigns* or *So Why Are We All Using Fertility? One Female Physician's Perspective* or *13 Bay*

Area Cancer Survivors Showcased as Sexy in the New Pinups for Purpose Calendar.

Complete product or program information should appear in the first two paragraphs. Direct quotes from industry experts or participants help embellish the release and add to the credibility of stories.

The last paragraph should include short, factual information about the company, product or service, and include the website. This is your "boiler-plate" statement and is included in everything you send out.

- **Photo(s).** High-resolution and professional photos are the best. Photos that portray action are preferable to the head-and-shoulders studio-type shots. Hire a professional photographer and ensure that the photography session includes a pre-planning consultation and photoshop services for easy touchups. You should also ask for high *and* low resolution photos—there will be occasions where you'll need both.

- **Company, product or service history.** This is a one-page document giving the facts and figures, or major selling information, as needed. It can include the inspiration behind creating the company, the philanthropic fundraising idea or annual events produced in the past. This makes it easy to scan the important facts, and adds the history and credibility.

- **Biography.** The bio gives the essential highlights of the individual's career contribution. It is factual— not promotional.

- **Testimonials.** Testimonials provide third-party endorsement, which create that know, like and trust factor for prospective clients. Create celebrity moments with your satisfied customers by capturing them on video, audio or print. Honor them by attaching their photos with the accolades in your promotional materials and website.

Professional Video

Always use a professional videographer. Arrange for professionally edited two-minute videos. Include advance scripting, testimonials, quality lighting and professional sound. Upload to YouTube® and your website.

Top Tips to Pitch Your News to the Media

- **Subject lines sell.** Make the subject line of your email pitch compelling. Make sure it reads like a good headline on the cover of a magazine, website or newspaper. Remember, reporters, producers and editors get hundreds of e-pitches a day, so make yours the one they want to open first! Stretch, be provocative.

- **Personalize the connection.** If you know the journalist or can make a personal pitch, that is best.

- **Know the audience.** Be sure you are talking about the media outlet's audience in the right way. If you are contacting a radio station, mention "listeners." For a TV station, "viewers" and for print "readers."

- **Copy and paste.** Copy and paste the text of your press release into the body of your email.

- **Just send text.** Get rid of all attached images, such as logos, photos, fancy photo signatures and so on, unless you have been specifically asked to send them. Follow up with an offer to provide additional images.

- **Press kits are powerful.** More and more people are avoiding email and once again enjoy postage mail. If you have a product, interesting materials or a book to share, mail a press kit. Focus on the media's needs for news and information, not just on your needs for advertising or promoting.

- **Use the media's tools and resources.** Just about every media outlet has a place on their website where you can upload or email press releases. If you cannot find the right person to send it to, call their main office and ask! Remember, what's in it for their particular audience?

- **Mornings are good.** Emailing before 10:00 a.m. is usually a perfect time. Many media folks are on deadline later in the day, rushing to finish stories. Sundays can also be a good time to break through all the noise and clutter in their inbox.

- **Wire services work.** If you need to make a national or global news announcement, consider using a wire service like PRNewswire, PR Web, Business Wire® or Vocus.

- **Be accurate and never stretch the truth!** Make sure everything is correct, check all hyperlinks, make sure your website is current. Build trust by always being accurate and truthful.

- **Partner with the media.** If you get in the door, respect their time and ask them if you can help them with anything else. Find out what kinds of experts they may need for future stories and then deliver.

You Got the Coverage—Now What?

Post the coverage in your media room on your website. Following the media exposure, be sure to send the journalist a note highlighting some key comments and interchanges. Compliment the story with specifics of your experience and mention accolades for the media personnel who were involved. Offer to share other ideas that may have appeal. Keep in touch, even when you are *not* promoting or selling something, be of service. In short, develop a sound media contact for the future.

Get Started Now

Needless to say, the disciplined approach to the fields of marketing, sales and public relations is ever evolving and changing. The impact of social media—too vast to include in this space—has had tremendous impact on each of these fields. We are now in the era of "citizen journalism" in a major way, and are still wading through that quagmire, with more to come.

If you have an inspirational idea, go for it. Look for ways to make a difference and get noticed. Always operate with integrity, and follow through. When you over deliver in customer service, clients will sing your praises.

For public relations media exposure, look for ways to leverage your product or services with current headlines. If it is with expert commentary on a breaking current news event, great. When press opportunities arise, respond immediately with credible business acumen.

You, as an entrepreneur, can be out there and be seen and heard, whether as a speaker, blogger, an e-zine writer/editor, on video or pod casting, on radio or TV interviews—whatever meets your sales, marketing and PR needs, go get the results. Talk about convergence. We have the world at our fingertips.

Special *Woman Entrepreneur Extraordinaire* Offer

If you are looking for creative ideas to gain more credibility, land media coverage or just want to explore creative ways that can help prospects find their reasons for buying from you, contact LynAnn for a complimentary 30-minute brainstorming session. In your email, provide a short summary of your business (promo) and expertise (bio) to give her advanced preparation for your session.

LYNANN KING
Marketing Visionary, Strategist, Publicist

(650) 550-0090
lynannking@kingsingspr.com
www.kingsingspr.com

LynAnn King partners with successful small businesses and empowers entrepreneurs to deliver authentic marketing communications, special events promotions and media campaigns. She brings her visionary leadership in rolling out creative marketing campaigns that create visibility and media coverage. Her clients are business-to-consumer in the luxury and aspirational markets, national speakers, nonprofits, national conferences, published authors, celebrity personalities and other professionals.

She served as vice president of marketing for the San Francisco chapter of The Association of Image Consultants International® (AICI) for five years and contributes on the international marketing committee promoting annual conferences. In 2005, she was honored as her chapter's member of the year. She has also served as publicist for the Marin Association of Female Executives, Pinups for Purpose, Dine Around/Passport Program and Professional Women's Chamber Connection. LynAnn is currently a member serving the board of Public Relations Society of America.

With a bachelor of science degree in business marketing from San Francisco State University, LynAnn had a successful career in high tech, performing arts and luxury sales before launching her boutique public relations and marketing company.

Getting It All Done and Loving It!
By Heather Calma, CPC

*B*enjamin Franklin once wrote, "Early to bed, early to rise, makes a man healthy, wealthy, and wise." This could not be more true.

Did you know most millionaires accomplish more by 8 a.m. than the average person accomplishes in an entire day? Think about your average day. Do you feel as if your family is demanding your attention, your business is going in ten different directions, and you cannot remember what free time really is?

I was once asked what I did in my free time, and my best answer was, "Sleep!" That was the day I realized I needed harmony among my business, my family, my faith and my much needed free time.

Many times, we feel guilty no matter what we are doing—especially if we are mothers. When we are playing with our children, we often think of the calls we should be making for our business, or when we are in a meeting, we have that inner voice telling us we should be spending time with the children.

As an entrepreneur, you have to be a professional plate spinner. Your attention is pulled everywhere. If you do not give proper attention to each task in your life, your life will quickly come crashing down just like the plates. I have found a way to create harmony by living by my core values, the Four P's, scheduling, learning to say no and by incorporating several other laws and principals. In this chapter, I will share my secrets for keeping the plates spinning, getting it all done and loving it.

Make Each Day a Masterpiece

Live each day with passion and purpose and make it a masterpiece. Ask yourself if you are living by your core values. The core values of your business are those values that form the foundation on which you perform work and conduct yourself. The core values are the basic elements of how you go about your work. They are the practices you use every day in everything you do. (See "From the Corporate World to Your Own World" by LaNette Parker on page 13.)

If you have not yet identified your core values, take a moment after reading this chapter to sit down and write down six values that are most important to you. Post this list where you will be reminded of these values each day.

I posted my core values on my vision board above my desk. My core values are balance, faith, family, success, calmness and achievement. I took these core values and created a morning mantra to speak to myself privately before I start each day. I recite, "When I balance faith, family and success with calmness, I reach achievement."

Throughout the day, I revisit my mantra and remind myself to live out the *Law of Magnetism*, which states that who you are is who you attract. What you want in people and what you get is not always a match. You attract people by what you are, not what you want. Be sure to surround yourself with likeminded people who will add value to your life. Find people who believe what you believe but who think different thoughts.

Make sure each activity you perform meets the Four P's:

- **Professionalism.** You are always presenting yourself in a professional manner.

- **Productivity.** You are accomplishing tasks, not just being busy.

- **Positivity.** You cannot have positive productivity with negativity.

- **Purpose.** Your every act has a purposeful intent.

If you catch yourself engaging in an activity that does not fall within the Four P's, ask yourself, "How is this enriching my life?" If you cannot give yourself a good answer, it is time to end that activity and begin a new activity that will add value to yourself or others.

Set a Schedule

My second child, Alex, is a very special child. He was a micro-preemie and required a lot of attention. Over the years, through this wonderful child, I learned how important a set schedule is. I learned the importance of adhering to business hours born of the need to balance my direct sales business with a family all while homeschooling.

Every part of your life—your business, family time, hobbies, meditation or prayer, additional schooling and so on—can be put on a schedule. Make appointments with yourself and always show up. For example, as I write this chapter, my schedule shows, "Work on co-author chapter." I am doing exactly what I scheduled myself to be doing at this moment. My phone is off. I am not being distracted. Most importantly, I am being productive and do not feel any guilt.

Learn to Say No

Most entrepreneurs are over-achievers and often find it hard to say "no" to all the opportunities that come their way. Being driven women, you like to think you can do anything that presents itself. However, you can only juggle so much at a time.

You know the old saying, "I really dropped the ball on that one." I'm not sure who originally came up with that, but I am pretty sure it must have been a woman. I have learned you must *slow down* in order to *speed up!* You must stay in control of your schedule and focus on the most important of tasks.

Follow the Pareto Principle

Activity is not necessarily accomplishment. In 1906, Italian economist Vilfredo Pareto observed that eighty percent of the land in Italy was owned by twenty percent of the population. He developed the principle by observing that twenty percent of the pea pods in his garden contained eighty percent of the peas. It has become a common rule of thumb in business that eighty percent of sales come from twenty percent of clients.

The Pareto Principle determines your effectiveness. Entrepreneurs love action and get excited about activity. However, it is really about *what you are accomplishing,* not *what are you doing.* This rule is not about getting the most things done. It is about getting the right things done.

Where is your time and energy going? Each day, take the ten most important tasks and prioritize them from one—most important—to ten—least important. If you only do the top two items, which is twenty percent of the list, they will give you an eighty percent return.

Do what you know is most important. Prioritize the items that will give you the greatest return.

This rule applies to your to-do list and to people. If you take the ten top people in your organization and rank them according to their contributions to the organization, and you put eighty percent of your time developing the top two people, 80% of what you need, you will get back. Focus on developing people who can lead—you cannot do everything yourself. As a leader, you have to be very careful how you prioritize with whom you spend your time and what tasks you are accomplishing. Remember, being busy is not the same as accomplishment. We are entrepreneurs, so, of course, we are busy. However, what is most important is what we are accomplishing.

Be Willing to Admit You Need Help

Once you are actively following the Pareto Principle, you may find some tasks need attention and not necessarily by you. I highly recommend you hire an assistant or a virtual assistant. This is something I struggled with for quite a while. I knew that in order to get it all done and to keep my sanity, I needed an assistant. However, I was not willing to give up control. Someone brought to my attention I was "dropping the ball" on a few things, and I learned how much value an assistant could bring to my business. I finally gave in and hired someone. (See also "Expand Your Business with an Effective Virtual Team" by Dortha Hise on page 165.)

I knew within the first week what a great decision I had made! In order to keep control, I gave her tasks that did not take my personal attention, such as sending cards, database work and so on. Once I realized what a blessing she was, I gave her more tasks, including booking appointments, doing follow-up calls and updating my social media sites. I do not know how I functioned without her.

If you cannot afford a high-quality assistant, start small, perhaps with a high school student to do envelope stuffing and mailing. Just having a little help with the mundane tasks can have a huge impact on your level of stress and, ultimately, will give you more time to "get it all done."

Stop Multitasking

The term *multitasking* was created for computers and refers to the ability to *execute* more than one task at the same time—a task in the computer world being a program.

We are not computers. We are women, and even though we may feel we are super human beings, in the end, we are just human beings. We were not designed to be computers and to work on many things at once.

When you are multitasking, you are not giving 100 percent of your thought and energy to the task. Many times, I hear a woman claim she is the "queen of multitasking," and I used to be envious. Sure, I could give a bottle to a baby, do the laundry and talk on the phone all at the same time. However, as a business woman, I could not seem to manage the act of multitasking and be successful. I tried and tried, and I honestly thought something was wrong with me because I could not seem to do it effectively. I quickly realized the reason I wasn't effective: I was not giving 100 percent.

As entrepreneurs, don't you always want to give 100 percent? Don't you always expect others to give you 100 percent attention? Why should you settle for giving less than 100 percent to your business and to the things that are going to give you the highest return?

When you stop multitasking, you are being present and engaged at all times. This will add value to your life and to your interactions with others. It also will give others the respect you would expect them to give to you.

Be Willing to Sacrifice

There is no success without sacrifice. If you want to *go up*, you have to *give up*. I remember early in my career in direct sales, I was invited to go on a trip with some friends. I really wanted to go on this trip, but I knew that I already had a prior commitment to a team member. At the time, my friends could not understand why I could not just reschedule—they did not understand why my business was so important to me. Looking back, I see that I did sacrifice quite a bit in the early days. Even today, I see that I am still missing events that would be enjoyable. However, in the end, success is what is important to me.

You must give up things to increase your value. There is no such thing as a successful entrepreneur who has not given something up to realize that success. When you begin your journey to greatness, you will need to eliminate excess baggage, such as unsupportive friends, drama and people who do not add value to your life. You cannot climb mountains with lots of things weighing you down.

What is success worth to you? It is not a one-time investment. You have to keep giving up in order to keep going up. You know you are on the road to success when it is an uphill journey the entire way. If you are coasting, you are heading in the wrong direction. People who are willing to pay the price and let go of that extra baggage are the ones who will reach the final destination.

How badly to do you really want to succeed? What are you willing to give up in order to accomplish what you want to accomplish?

Make It a Family Enterprise

Involve your children and family in your business, so when the going is good, the family enjoys the success, too. I will never forget the first project my children helped me with. I refer to this as "rocks in bags." To this day, if I mention "rocks in bags," my oldest son, Chance, just giggles.

When I was very new to direct sales, I wanted an inexpensive way to get my name out there, and I was going to do whatever it took. I came up with the idea of making fliers, putting them in newspaper sleeves, adding a rock for weight and throwing them in people's driveways. I am an overachiever, so 100 flyers were not going to cut it—neither was 200. In the end, my children and I stuffed and tossed more than 1,000 bags into driveways across town. This process took about four days to complete and when that phone started ringing, we would all squeal with excitement! I am still doing repeat business with some of those clients we originally found through the "rocks-in-bags" project.

My children know they helped me with something that is still providing income for the family. This gives them a feeling of excitement and accomplishment. If you have small children, they can be involved with things as well. My daughter Aurora loves stickers, so I always let her put stickers on my envelopes, order forms and so on. The only rule is that the sticker must be somewhat straight and completely on the paper. By involving your children, you are creating a foundation for them and an understanding of business. I do not expect all four of my children to follow in my footsteps, but I know that when they are older, they will remember the fun we had as a family working together.

Be Flexible

So what happens if you do not get it all done or things do not go exactly as planned? In 2009, my life took a dramatic change after the birth of my fourth premature baby, Enzo. (Every one of my children was born seven to nine weeks early!)

My faith is very important to me. I believe my agenda may not necessarily be God's agenda. Each morning, I take time to sit on my dock and center myself. I keep my mind open to accept what the Lord has for me to do today. As I mentioned before when I spoke about needing to hire an assistant, I had a hard time giving up control. However, I have found that by giving up control and following God's plan for me, I am able to accomplish more than I ever thought was possible.

If prayer is not your path, try meditation or just sitting in silence for a while each morning to get centered and focused on what you need to do that day.

I adhere to a schedule, plan my day and prioritize. I also know I have to be open to distractions that may come my way. Years ago, I would become upset over distractions. Today, I have learned to find a gift in everything. A distraction is not the end of the world, and it will not kill you. It just opens the door to a new opportunity. Embrace change and distractions. We are women, we are amazing, and it is okay if it does not all get done, at least for today.

Special *Woman Entrepreneur Extraordinaire* Offer

I would like to offer you a *free*, 45-minute coaching session to become acquainted. I can show you first-hand the power of coaching by letting you experience it around a particular area or topic. Please email me at heather@heathercalma.com with code *WEE* to redeem this offer.

HEATHER CALMA, CPC

(561) 317-4919
heather@heathercalma.com
www.heathercalma.com

Heather Calma is a certified John C. Maxwell® trainer, speaker and business coach with nine years of direct sales experience. She was a top sales producer and the national director of a one-million-dollar sales organization. Heather has spoken at several national conventions on the topic of organization, maintaining healthy business relationships, increasing sales, the art of sponsoring and has served on her company's advisory board for several years. She has received many awards, including the Top Sales Performer and Number One in Sponsoring.

Heather believes it does not matter what background you come from—it only matters where you are going! She teaches others to release the past and start reaching for success in the future. She speaks and empowers individuals to succeed no matter their backgrounds and helps her clients eliminate negative thoughts and anything that gets in the way of success.

Today, Heather leads a successful coaching business with clients from all over the globe while residing in Palm Beach Gardens, Florida, with her 4 children, husband, Marc, and dog, Ruby.

Break Free to Six Figures
Seven Keys to Create a Six-Figure Business in Twelve Months or Less
By Georgina Sweeney

Did you know that 87 percent of women-owned firms earn less than $100,000? It's true according to *Mapping the "Missing Middle": Determining the Desire and Dimensions of Second-Stage Women Business Owners,* published May 2007 by Womenable, a for-profit social enterprise that works to enable women's entrepreneurship worldwide. Yet, it does not have to be that way! If you are not enjoying the success and wealth you desire, here are seven key strategies I personally use that will help you build a *six-figure business in twelve months or less.*

Strategy One: Clear the Way for Success

> *"I tell you that as long as I can conceive something better than myself I cannot be easy unless I am striving to bring it into existence or clearing the way for it."*
> —George Bernard Shaw, Irish playwright

To arrive at any destination quickly, it helps to know your starting point, have clear directions and be aware of any roadblocks along the way. The same principles apply when creating a six-figure business. Time spent mapping out your future, evaluating your current position and understanding what business and personal blocks may be holding you back will allow you to stay on course and achieve your six-figure goals.

Action One: Assess your current situation. I invite you to take a few moments now to assess where you are in your current business and determine what is working and not working for you. If you need help with this step, consider hiring a business coach or take advantage of free resources provided by the Small Business Administration (SBA) or the Service Corps of Retired Executives (SCORE) in the United States. Some key areas you might like to review are:

• Overall vision and business strategy

• Target market and niche

• Branding and messaging

• Products and services

• Sales and pricing strategy

• Online and offline marketing and communication plans

• Client attraction and retention

• Business and professional skills

• Technical and organizational skills

• Resources and support

Once you have determined the areas that need your immediate attention, decide what specific actions you are going to take in the next thirty days to address them. The goal is to quickly fix what may be broken, so you can move on to the next stage of wealth creation.

Action Two: Uncover your personal blocks to success. Perhaps more limiting than business blocks are the personal fears, doubts and negative beliefs that consciously or unconsciously sabotage our success, such as:

- "I'm not good enough."

- "I don't know enough."

- "I can't charge that much."

Every day we tell ourselves stories that are just not true. How do I know this? I have told myself those same stories, and I have listened to my clients repeat them, too. Not surprisingly, as soon as I released them, my business took off, and I have not looked back since.

Although I use a variety of techniques to identify and dissolve blocks, one of the fastest and easiest methods is to simply ask yourself the following questions and wait for your inner voice to respond:

- What is the number one thing you are avoiding or resisting doing in your business that, if you did it now, would help you move forward quickly and be more successful?

- What is the pain, fear or discomfort you associate with taking that action?

- What are the positives associated with not taking action?

- What is the negative consequence of not taking action?

- How will you benefit by taking action now?

- What specific action will you decide to take within the next week to overcome this resistance and help move you forward with your business goals?

Although deceptively simple, these questions will soon have you back in action if you are feeling stuck. (See "Master the Secrets for Entrepreneurial Success" by Beverly Lenz on page 49.)

My shortcut to success. Before taking a specific action—for example, public speaking or raising my fees—I check in with myself and see if I feel any resistance in my mind or body to moving forward. If I do, I use Emotional Freedom Techniques® (EFT), a new discovery that combines ancient Chinese acupressure with modern psychology, to quickly dissolve any resistance and allow me to be immediately successful. Try it and let me know if it works for you! (See "Rapid Business Growth for Financial Freedom" by Arlene Krantz on page 85 for more about EFT.)

Strategy Two: Monetize Your Talents

"Talent is like electricity.
We don't understand electricity. We use it."
—Maya Angelou, African-American author and poet

Doing what comes naturally to you and inspires you is not only enjoyable, it is also a key for creating a six-figure business and sustaining success. Although your talents and gifts may seem of little value to you, those around you are often willing to invest large sums of money to access or learn those skills, especially if they help solve a pressing problem.

If you are not aware of your unique talents, the following questions may be of use to you in identifying and later monetizing them:

- Think about your individual talents. What can you do that comes easily or naturally to you that other people struggle with?

- What do people naturally come to you for help with?

- What compliments do people pay you?

- What do you love to spend time doing that lights you up and that you can easily talk about or read about for hours?

- If you won the lottery and money was no longer an object or an issue for you, and there were no additional constraints placed upon you, what would you do with your newfound freedom and resources that had meaning for you?

The answers to these questions may guide you in a new business direction or simply give you ideas for new products and services. Be sure to keep them in mind as we discuss Strategy #3. (See "From Passion to Success" by Simone Hoa on page 25.)

My shortcut to success. For several years, I operated two successful, separate businesses—one dedicated to energy work and the other dedicated to business coaching. I knew intuitively I should combine them. However, I feared my business clients would not take me seriously if I did. I need not have worried because as soon as I combined all my talents and incorporated energy work and mindset mastery into my business coaching, I quadrupled my success almost overnight! What talents do you possess that do not appear to mix? How can you combine them for greater success and personal satisfaction?

Strategy Three: Choose a Hungry and Emotional Crowd

"I cannot give you the formula for success,
but I can give you the formula for failure, which is:
try to please everybody."
–Herbert Bayard Swope, American editor and journalist

If you have been in business for any amount of time, you will most likely have heard the term "niche." According to www.businessdictionary.com, a market niche is, "A small but profitable segment of a market suitable for focused attention by a marketer."

In order to build a six-figure business, I encourage you to choose a well-defined niche and within it, a *hungry and emotional crowd.* This is a group of people who are actively searching for a solution to a burning problem that affects them emotionally. The following example helps illustrate this:

- **Market:** People who want to lose weight

- **Niche:** Women who want to lose weight

- **Hungry and Emotional Crowd:** Brides who want to lose their last ten, stubborn pounds before their wedding

My shortcut to success. I choose my *hungry and emotional crowd* by first examining my own pressing problems and desires, as well as who I am, my defining personality traits, my values, my interests, my deepest desires. Then I find groups of people who also fit this description. By easily identifying with my "crowd," I can build instant rapport with them and create effective programs and solutions with little effort. Who is your hungry and emotional crowd?

Strategy Four: Offer Differentiated Value

"Let no one ever come to you without leaving better and happier."
—Mother Teresa, Albanian missionary
and Nobel Peace Prize® winner

We have finally arrived at the cornerstone of wealth—ensuring you first provide value for others. This does not mean discounting your prices. Quite the opposite! When you market your products and services based on pricing alone, potential clients will inevitably shop around, or your competitors will match your prices, leaving you little room for success. However, if you package your products and services into results-based, high-value solutions that satisfy the most pressing needs of your *hungry and emotional crowd,* you will immediately differentiate yourself in the marketplace, be seen as the specialist solution to your niche's problems and be able to command higher prices overnight.

My shortcut to success. One of my strengths is to create rapid breakthroughs and results for my clients. I capitalized on this strength by creating a ninety-day cash explosion secrets program that included a guarantee. This combination of fast, guaranteed results allowed me to immediately double my fees and sign up clients effortlessly. What differentiated value can you create today?

Strategy Five: Break Through Your Money Blocks and Charge What You Are Worth

"The minute you settle for less than you deserve,
you get even less than you settled for."
—Maureen Dowd, American newspaper columnist

There may be another reason why you have not yet reached six figures. Maybe you have not dared to charge what you are worth. Limited self-worth often finds its roots in childhood, where we may have been exposed for many years to negative money beliefs held by our friends and family, as well as negative personal experiences that have left an imprint on our unconscious mind and continue to influence our actions today.

The following table, "Common Limiting Beliefs & Negative Imprints," lists some common limiting beliefs and negative "imprints," as I like to call them. See if any of them resonate with you. If they do, be sure to transform them, as well as the personal blocks you uncovered in Strategy #1, using EFT or mindset coaching, so you can finally charge what you are worth.

COMMON LIMITING BELIEFS & NEGATIVE IMPRINTS	A I do not hold this belief	B I hold this belief somewhat	C I hold this belief strongly	D I hold this belief very strongly and know it's keeping me from success
You have to work hard to have money or be successful.				
Money is hard to manage.				
Wealthy people are greedy.				
Money doesn't bring happiness.				
I can't make money doing what I love.				
I don't know enough.				
I'm not smart enough.				
I'm not good enough.				
I can't charge that much.				
I'm afraid to fail.				
If I'm successful, people will not like me.				
I feel guilty about having money.				
Spiritual people aren't supposed to have money.				

My shortcut to success. As mentioned earlier, I use EFT to release limiting beliefs and blocks. I also use positive affirmations to program the thoughts that I would like to have instead. What new thoughts and beliefs are you ready to embrace?

Strategy Six: Master the Art of Heart-Centered Selling

> *"The mind gives us a thousand ways to say no, but there's only one way to say yes, and that's from the heart."*
>
> —Suze Orman, American Personal Finance Expert

If the idea of having a sales conversation makes you feel uncomfortable, I invite you to consider the following.

Selling is simply an opportunity to enter into a heart-centered conversation with a qualified prospect to understand their needs, learn whether you can be of service to them and determine if you are a mutually ideal match.

When you lead with your head or allow your ego to guide you, you may tend to focus on "closing the sale" with your attention placed solely on you and your needs, not on those of your potential client. When you speak from the heart, however, the sales conversation becomes effortless and results in greater success and less stress. By following a heart-centered sales approach, I enjoy a ninety-percent success rate or higher. Here are some of my top tips.

- **Let go of any attachment to the outcome.** When you let go of any attachment to the outcome and focus solely on listening and providing value for your prospect, you will relax into the conversation and allow both of you to discover whether you are a good fit.

- **Spend time helping your prospect clarify their needs and wants.** If you take the time to help your prospect clarify their needs and understand where they are today, where they want to go and what is stopping them from getting there, they will often experience a mini-breakthrough during the sales conversation. This helps to position you as an expert and gives them a taste of what using your products or working with you will be like, increasing your odds of sales success. (See "Customer Service Cuts through Competition" by Sheri Brunnquell on page 131 for more information on this.)

- **Be prepared to walk away.** One of the most empowering and financially rewarding decisions you can make in your business is to consciously choose your clients, rather than simply allow them to choose you. When you work exclusively with ideal clients who excite and inspire you, you will find that you naturally deliver your finest work day after day, which, in turn, produces great results and leads to increased referrals. As you engage in conversation with your prospects, ask yourself whether they are ideal for you. Listen to your intuition and be prepared to walk away if they are not. If they are, be sure to let them know how much you would enjoy working with them and invite them to become your client.

My shortcut to success. The key to getting a client is to help them see that you are the best solution to their problem. To help me do that, I invite qualified prospects to join me in a free thirty-minute discovery session where we discuss their situation one-on-one. I also ask them to complete a confidential questionnaire ahead of time to allow me get up to speed on their situation and begin assessing their problem. By the time they join me on the call, I already have solutions in mind that I share freely, giving the prospect confidence in my abilities to help them. What's your shortcut to sales success?

Strategy Seven: Create Multiple Streams of Income

"We are beginning to open up both individually and collectively to the realization that it is time to create our lives and our world differently."
—Shakti Gawain, American pioneer in the field
of personal development

Congratulations! By now, you should be earning or be close to earning six figures. The final step is to create multiple streams of income, including passive revenue, so you can enjoy more time and freedom in your life and make money even while you sleep.

Rather than work exclusively with clients one-on-one, think of ways you can package your time and expertise to benefit many. Group coaching programs, information products, CDs, video training courses, ebooks, membership sites and so on are all ways to monetize your expertise with minimal impact on your free time. (See "Information Products Equal Accelerated Cash Flow" by Michele Scism on page 155.)

My shortcut to success. Anytime I work with a new client or group, I document what I do so that I can systematize my process for the next client or group. This has helped me create several signature systems that allow me to differentiate my services and be paid for results and not time. How will you leverage your time and expertise for greater freedom and success?

Take Inspired Action!

We have covered a lot of ground in these seven strategies. Some of them may be new to you, and some may be familiar. What is important is to take inspired action and follow through on at least one strategy you can implement in your business quickly and easily.

Rest assured, wherever you are in your business, with just a few tweaks to your business model and your mindset, you can break free to six figures and beyond.

Special *Woman Entrepreneur Extraordinaire* Offer

Ready to take your business to the next level?

As a thank you for reading this chapter, please accept my free gift of a thirty-minute "Break Free to Six Figures" strategy session. Simply mention this book when you contact me. I guarantee you'll have at least one breakthrough during our call!

GEORGINA SWEENEY
Transformational Business Coach and
Money Mentor for Heart-Centered
Women Entrepreneurs

Create your own freedom ... NOW!

(207) 766-6058
georgina@georginasweeney.com
www.georginasweeney.com

Georgina Sweeney helps heart-centered women entrepreneurs create their own freedom—the freedom to be who they are, do what they love and earn what they want—now. She is the creator of *Cash Explosion Secrets: How to create an explosion of cash, opportunities and momentum in your business in 90 days or less and Break Free to Six Figures,* her signature coaching program that teaches women how to build a six-figure business in twelve months or even four months as she did.

Georgina is passionate about empowering women to listen to the call of their heart, make the difference they want to make in the world and enjoy the personal and financial freedom they deserve. Guided by her unique blend of strategic and imaginative marketing, inspirational business coaching, liberating energy work and heightened sense of intuition, her clients are amazed at the speed at which they achieve breakthroughs and success as they release old patterns of behavior, overcome their money blocks and get into action quickly.

A teacher, speaker and coach, Georgina lives in upstate New York where she and her husband are eagerly waiting to adopt a child.

Become a Sought After Speaker and Make Your Business Thrive!

By Caterina Rando, MA, MCC

*C*an you imagine walking out of your house in the morning, driving to a hotel in your community, giving a presentation to a room full of your potential clients whom you have never spoken to or met before and coming home the same afternoon with several new clients—what could be better? Note, I did not say the "possibility of new clients." I said "new clients"—people who were thrilled to sign up to work with you as soon as your presentation was concluded.

The reason not everyone is using public speaking to grow their business is because most people are afraid of public speaking and, therefore, avoid it at all costs. If you like to speak—or even if you are willing to speak—you will find it a highly effective way to attract new clients, build your email list and attract new opportunities. When you deliver a speech, it is as if you are having an introductory phone call or an initial appointment with a whole room full of people all at once, all potential clients.

Here are twelve important reasons why you want to start to become a sought-after speaker today.

1. Become Recognized as an Expert in Your Field

When your name is on the event flyer and you are standing in the front of a room speaking on a topic, the audience members assume you are an expert on that topic. The more potential clients perceive you as an expert, the more likely they are to do business with you.

2. Meet More People Faster

People do business with people they know, like and trust. Speaking gives several people an opportunity to get to know you all at once. When anyone in your audience needs the services you provide, they will be more likely to call you. They have already met you and have begun to know you, like you and trust you because they received value from your presentation.

3. Educate Potential Clients

When you speak to promote your business, you have an opportunity to educate the audience about your industry and your business. People will know about the services you provide, what kinds of clients you work with, and what a client can expect from you. This can save you a lot of phone time and help you to pre-qualify people who are considering working with you.

4. Create New Opportunities

Speaking will allow you to go before groups of people whom you may not otherwise meet. This can help you expand your sphere of influence, build your permission-based email list and provide you with a variety of new opportunities. The more people you deliver a speech to, the more opportunities for more speeches, writing, and being a guest on radio and television will come your way.

5. Meet Other Experts and Leaders

Speaking allows you to meet other successful people in your industry. One day, you may find yourself on the platform with the person you admire most. What could be better than that? Always be gracious and generous with your time and acknowledge others for their accomplishments and their presentation. The other people you meet on the platform can be great referral sources and strategic alliance partners for you in your business.

6. Attract More Clients, Contracts and Commissions

Speaking can be far more cost effective than advertising, direct mail, networking, cold calling and even social media. The rate of return on the time investment you make to prepare for and deliver a speech could turn out to be the smartest action you could take to generate new business. If you have a strong delivery and give a high content speech, you could leave with at least one new client every time you speak. Sometimes, you could come home with ten or twenty new clients—that sure makes for a good day of speaking.

7. Gain Increased Visibility

Whenever you are in the front of a room speaking to a group, you are being noticed. People will remember who you are and what your business does. The more people see you and see your business name, the more successful people think you are. Usually, when you speak to a group, the group publicizes the event. Many people who do not attend the event will still read the information about your business and may give you a call. Even if people do not call you, know that the more people who read your name and see your picture, the more they will feel comfortable with you and begin to trust you for future business dealings.

8. Keep in Touch with the Public

Speaking keeps you in touch and keeps you on your toes. It allows you to discover what issues are of concern to the people in your audiences. Then, you can address these concerns in your articles, videos and blogs and on your website. Also, when you get out of your office and connect with new people, they ask you questions and your opinion on topics you have not yet addressed. This can result in new ideas for new products and services for your company.

9. Enhance Your Own Personal and Professional Growth

When you go to different groups, meetings and conferences as a guest speaker, you will have many opportunities to hear other presenters on a variety of topics. Not only will this expand your network, you will learn a lot while keeping current on a variety of topics. This is always energizing, and you may come home with an idea that will transform your business and uplift your life.

10. Enjoy Perks, Perks and More Perks

As a guest speaker, sometimes you are gifted with nothing from the group that hosts you. Sometimes, you come home with a mug, a letter opener or a paperweight, and sometimes, you come home with beautiful flowers, dinner certificates and gift baskets. Also, when you become really well known as a speaker, you can be offered opportunities to speak on cruises, at fancy resorts and spas, and even at exotic destinations—all expenses paid.

11. Build a Better List, Better and Faster

When you go to speak to a group, the people in that group have a personal and positive experience with you, and you are beginning to build a relationship with them. When you do a drawing or offer them a discount if they give you their email address, you are building your list. This is one of the key objectives you have as a business owner. You always want to be building your list.

12. Get More Money Later

Many people will be impressed with you when you speak, and they may be interested in what you have to offer. They may not, however, be ready to hire you right now. By staying in touch with them through email, you will find that some people will come back to you later when they need what you have to offer.

Ten Steps to Becoming a Sought After Speaker

It should be very clear to you now that public speaking is definitely a solid way to catapult your business forward. If you are not convinced or ready to start, go back and read the previous section again.

I have been teaching entrepreneurs how to build their businesses with public speaking at an event called *The Sought After Speaker Summit*. I could easily fill this whole chapter with success stories of people just like you who have doubled and tripled their revenue with public speaking. There is Dana Lynch, an image professional, who started giving speeches at local department stores and always picked up new clients. There is Christine Giri, a productivity expert, who started doing tele-seminars for professional organizers and significantly grew her business. Tiffany Nielsen, a business etiquette trainer, started to speak to business groups in her community, and, as a result, her training business is busier than ever.

Follow these ten steps to get in front of your next clients and watch your business thrive.

Step One: Define Your Audience

To decide which groups you want to speak to, first think about who your ideal clients and strategic alliance partners are. Are they stay-at-home moms, homeowners, life coaches, property managers?

Identify who your ideal clients are, so you can follow the steps in this system with your ideal clients in mind and get in front of them.

Step Two: Get Your Speaker Sheet Done

Before you start to contact groups to be selected as a speaker, you need to have a marketing PDF that positions you as a speaker. It lets the decision maker for a group know the topic you want to present on and the benefits the audience will receive when they listen to your speech. Your speaker sheet will make you look like a speaker and make you appear experienced, even if you are just getting started. You cannot get booked as a speaker if you do not look like one.

Here are a few things to keep in mind when creating your speaker sheet. Be sure to include:

- A catchy, benefit-focused title at the top like, *Financial Secrets for Women Revealed* or *Successful Communication Strategies* or *Real Estate Buying Secrets for the Savvy Investor.*

- A bio that describes you as a speaker. This is not your usual bio. Add words and phrases about your speaking style, for example, "down-to-earth," "practical," "dynamic" or "knowledgeable."

- A professional color photo of you. Make sure it is recent and of high quality, and that you look very happy in the picture.

- Your contact information, including your phone number and email address and website. Be easy to get in touch with.

Step Three: Create Your Criteria

I want you to get great business-building results from each speech you deliver. Therefore, before you say "yes" to deliver a speech, there are some important questions to answer to ensure you are setting yourself up for maximum success every time you present:

- Who will be in the audience? Remember, you want to speak to audiences where your ideal clients are gathered.

- How many people will be in the audience? I never met a program chair who gave me an accurate count for how many people would be in attendance. You can figure at least ten fewer than you are told. You may not want to drive a long way to present to only a few people.

- How long is the maximum time you can present? Regardless of how much time they offer you, you ask for more. Because the more time people spend with you, the more they get to know you, and the more money they will be willing to invest with you.

- Can I take a few minutes toward the end to let the audience know about my offerings? If the answer is "no" to this question, I strongly suggest you decline the opportunity unless they can spring for a generous honorarium. In other words, if they say "no," do not go.

Step Four: Identify the Right Groups for You and Build a Target List

You cannot reach out to any group to speak if you do not know whom to contact. Identify the right groups to present to and build a list of those groups. Include the following information in your list:

- Website address for the group

- Where they meet

- When they meet

- How many people attend their meetings or events

- The name of the contact person in charge of booking speakers

- The phone number of the contact person

- The email of the contact person

- Any notes about the group, like someone you know who belongs to the group, what is it about the group that makes you interested in presenting there, if you have ever been to the group before. Perhaps you know someone who has presented to the group and you can ask about their experience.

Step Five: Connect with Your Target Groups

When you know whom to contact, reach out and offer yourself as a speaker. After you have your speaker sheet, send an email to the contact person for the groups on your list and write something like this:

Dear _____,

I am thrilled to learn about the Savvy Businesswomen Association [or the name of whatever group you are reaching out to] that meets in Happytown on Tuesdays. ([location and day of the regular meetings]

You are listed as the program chair on the website. I have a great program on using speaking to grow your business [your topic] that would be very beneficial to your group's members. Please let me know if you're interested in discussing having me deliver a presentation for one of your upcoming meetings.

Attached is more information on my most popular presentations for your review.

I welcome the opportunity to discuss presenting to your group.

Sincerely,
[Your name]
[Your phone]
[Your email address]
[Your website]

Step Six: Continue to Follow Up

Be aware, most groups are run by volunteers and often change leadership every year. This means it can take some calls and a little detective work to find the right person. Your best bet is a personal contact who can point you in the right direction and vouch for you as a speaker.

Step Seven: Be Loud and Proud that You Are a Speaker

It does you no good to decide you want to use speaking to promote your business if no one knows you are a speaker. Be loud and proud about who you are and the value you bring. Let people know you are speaking and send out an email to your list announcing your programs. Use social media to get the word out. Ask often to get booked.

Step Eight: Be an Awesome Speaker

The truth is that when you are a good speaker and do a good job of providing value to the audience, they will always refer you to other groups and be thrilled to have you back again soon. I believe in practicing your speaking skills in front of a real live audience, getting feedback from speakers you admire and investing in training to get better. There is always room to be a more awesome speaker.

Step Nine: Use an Offer Sheet to Easily Attract New Clients

Your speech is just a lot of excellent information if you do not ask the audience to become your clients. Always have an offer sheet and take time to go over your offer sheet to ensure you come home with business. Tell your audience you want to work with them and let them know how to get started.

Step Ten: Expect Success!

It can take time to get booked for speeches. It can take time to become an awesome speaker. It can take time to have those speeches turn into lots of business. Every day and every step of the way, it is important for you to expect you can effectively and successfully use public speaking to build a more thriving business.

Stay focused, take action and maintain your expect-success attitude. Soon, you will find you can accomplish your goal of becoming a sought-after speaker.

Special *Woman Entrepreneur Extraordinaire* Offer:

You get a bonus for reading all the way to the end of my chapter. Visit www.soughtafterspeaker.com and type in coupon code SASVIP50 to enjoy a 50% discount to attend our next event.

CATERINA RANDO, MA, MCC
Business Strategist, Speaker, Publisher

Making you and your business thrive

(415) 668-4535
cat@caterinarando.com
www.soughtafterspeaker.com
www.caterinarando.com
www.thrivebooks.com

Caterina Rando's mission is to show entrepreneurs how to build thriving businesses. She is a sought-after speaker, business strategist and author of the national bestseller, *Learn to Power Think,* from Chronicle Books. Caterina is co-author of *Direct Selling Power, Incredible Business* and *Make Your Connections Count,* all from THRIVE Publishing™. She is also featured as a success expert in several other leading business books including: *Build It Big, Get Clients Now* and *Get Slightly Famous.*

Since 1993, Caterina has been providing consulting, training and solutions to ensure women entrepreneurs succeed. Through her Business Breakthrough Summit, Sought After Speaker Summit and Social Media Marketing Summit for Women in Business, she and her team show women how to become recognized as experts, think and plan strategically and significantly grow their revenue. She is also the founder of THRIVE Publishing, a company that publishes books, including this book, for experts who want to share their message with a greater market.

Caterina holds a bachelor of science degree in organizational behavior and a master of arts degree in life transitions counseling psychology. She is a certified personal and professional coach (CPPC) and a master certified coach (MCC), the highest designation awarded by the International Coaching Federation®.

Networking and Creating Referral Partners

By Jeanie Breisinger

*H*ow did I get where I am today?

People see me as a *great networker*, which surprises me! I came from a small town and was always timid and shy. I never thought I would be a network marketer and a managing director of the most sought-after women's networking group in the United States. Yet, when I look at my career in pharmaceutical sales and my business life, most of my advancements have come from a referral or networking. Doors opened that I never thought were imaginable. In this chapter, I am honored to give you my secrets for networking that have catapulted my business life. I am going to show you how I have built lifelong connections with colleagues, friends and mentors. I will share how I have gotten a flood of clients and business though strategic networking.

Even with the Internet and social media, networking and personal connections have gotten me further and faster than anything else has. Real people contacting with real people is where magic happens. Real people are the foundation of any business. The face-to-face meeting and the handshake are where the true connections take place, deals are done and relationships are made for life.

Have you gone to a networking meeting, walked into a room and had someone try to sell you something from hello? I bet you felt as if you had walked onto a bad used car commercial where everyone was out to get your business!

While networking is not easy, it can be easily taught. Did you know that the secret is not about *you?* It is about *them.* As soon as I mastered this important fact, I gained lifelong friendships and business connections. Knowing this earlier would have saved me from many embarrassing moments.

I learned this very quickly in my pharmaceutical sales business. I was right out of training and bursting with technical knowledge. I had just finished studying and testing for some pharmaceutical products, was certified and was ready to share my knowledge with the physicians in my territory. I was about to meet with a physician prospect, and as soon as he walked over to me, I found myself blurting out every statistic, study and product blurb I had learned. Did I even say hello? No! The doctor just nodded, pretended to pay attention and backed away as fast as he could to see his next patient behind room four.

Had I influenced him, or had I embarrassed myself? You know the answer. I have definitely fallen down many times since then and have picked myself up just as many times. Why? Because in my corporate life, I knew I had to. If I did not, I did not have a job. I had to make this work. It forced me to gain the skills to build the relationships that have carried me to this day into my own business as a successful woman entrepreneur.

I am going to share these skills with you in this chapter, so you can avoid the embarrassment and mistakes I made to get here.

The More You Talk, the Less You Will Make

That is right. Are you thinking if you are not talking, how can you engage with the other person? After you introduce yourself, I always ask, "Tell me about you and your business." Then I close my mouth and listen. That's it. After I know more about the other person, I can usually add, "I know someone who needs to know about you and you need to meet." Instantly, we have a connection. I put them in contact with someone who would complement their business or who needs their services. This makes me a *connector*.

Become a Connector

When you are a connector, you are viewed as a *partner*, instead of a business card pusher. You connect the dots from what someone needs to someone who can meet that need. Before you know it, the wheel turns, and someone is connecting you with someone who needs what you offer. There is *your* opportunity. So, become a connector.

Here is an example: I was recently heading for Sacramento, California, to work with a team member. Before going, I attended a networking group where I connected with a woman business owner in Sacramento. I told her that I would love to connect with her when I was visiting her area, and I knew quite a few contacts that she needed to connect with who could help her in her business. I set the appointment, met with her and created an unbelievable connection. For more than an hour, we discussed her business, and I gave her a laundry list of people she could connect with. She asked about my business, and we ended by setting up a time to re-connect by phone and follow up with one another.

In my eyes, we are all connected, and it takes just one person to bring us all together. That is it! (See the chapter "It's Not Stalking... It's Follow Up!" by Elizabeth McCormick on page 143.)

Know Your Target Market

This was the hardest thing for me to do when I left corporate America. I always received a list to focus on, and I was great at working my list. However, in the entrepreneur world, the list is the list *you* create. Whatever your product is, there is a specific market for it. The more fine-tuned you are in defining your market, the better.

There is a reason why the ketchup is next to the mustard in the grocery store or the peanut butter is next to the jelly. People who want one also want the other.

Around the Fourth of July, does your local grocery store have a display for barbeque foods and accessories? Now, you will see the ketchup and mustard on display next to the charcoal and beer. Sales will increase quite a bit during this season because the grocer knows what his or her customers want and makes it easy for them to buy.

What does ketchup and mustard have to do with your business?

Study your market, so you know specifically what your customers need in order to drive business. The more you know about your customers, such as age, sex and demographic information, the better you can communicate with them and meet their needs.

This is my target market. The clients I want to work with fit this description: *A woman age 40-59 who has her own business in coaching or sales and whose client retention and referrals have decreased. She needs referrals to increase her profits and needs to build relationships with her clients.*

Can you define your customers this clearly? If not, here are some questions to help you focus:

- Who would use your product?

- What would you tell other people about your product?

- What do you like most about the product's features and benefits?

(See also "Think like a CEO" by Alice Hinckley on page 37.)

Find the Bright Stars

Bright stars are centers of influence. They stand out as leaders, have good relationships and develop a following. They light the way for others, and people naturally gravitate toward them. Bright stars get more business more easily. Not only this, they help *others* get more business more easily.

Why do some people work hard with only a few clients and struggle financially, then they meet someone and suddenly everything turns around? This new acquaintance is a *center of influence*—a bright star—who inspires and motivates through their actions, communication examples and connections. Bright stars shine and are the center of the galaxy. One way I have found the center of influence is by asking. Ask, "Who do you know? I am trying to do (fill in the blank) and I don't know who to talk to."

Once you find the key center of influence, I would ask about his or her opinion of your product or service. Could they use it? I am not shy about sharing my goals. I will say something like, "I am working on launching this business and I am looking for other people to help me spread the word; do you know anyone or anyone they know who could help me?"

Whom do you know—or want to know—who could be a center of influence for you? What are you going to do to get into orbit around them? What would it take you to become a center of influence?

Make Friends with Gatekeepers

The gatekeeper is someone who stands between you and your prospect or center of influence. Gatekeepers are valuable resources for the person you are trying to reach, and they are the key to your reaching that person.

Most likely, the gatekeeper controls the calendar, answers the phones and has the backstage pass to the person you need to reach. I treat gatekeepers as if *they* are centers of influence. I get to know them. I make small talk, pay attention to their needs, send thank you cards and so on. This has gained me access to physicians—who can be almost impossible to meet with—and multi-million-dollar entrepreneurs. I have gotten business, joined their networks and discovered great referral partners.

What can you do to cultivate the gatekeepers who stand between you and the centers of influence you need to meet?

Do Your Homework to Meet the Right People

If you are going to an event, plan whom you want to meet and do research. How many times have you paid for an event and just showed up hoping to make valuable connections? How often have you come home with sore feet and no contacts?

What if you research the event before you arrive and decide whom you want to meet? Maybe it is one of the speakers. You could do some research on this speaker's website or search for them on Google®. You would know exactly what to talk about. You would feel comfortable meeting them because you are prepared, and you can create instant rapport and connection with them. Doors will open to his or her network, which is huge! (See "Become a Sought After Speaker and Make Your Business Thrive!" by Caterina Rando on page 221.)

238

Do not stop now! Before you leave, make appointments or plans to meet with them and other potential clients. I have done this, and it works like a charm. It gives me the opportunity to get to know people away from the crowd and see how I can help them. I recently did this, and it brought in not only more referrals, but also an entirely new network. Just from this *one* get-together, I was introduced to people whom I could never have otherwise met.

Get Referrals

Ask. If you are struggling with referrals or growing your client database, send a referral letter. I learned this from James Roche, head coach of the Millionaire Protégé Club™ with Ali Brown. Ali Brown was recently featured in ABC's *Secret Millionaire*® and has fast become regarded as the voice for women's entrepreneurial success. As founder and CEO of Ali International LLC, she has created a dynamic enterprise that is devoted to empowering women entrepreneurs around the world and currently has over 50,000 members in her online and offline programs. James is brilliant. He is big about increasing referrals through a referral system, and it works like a charm. James' advice is to send a warm referral letter out to your current clients, family and friends and mention your business and a few key points, such as who is a perfect client for your services. Tell them they will receive a reward for sending a referral. This tip has helped many people increase their client list.

If you do not ask, you will not receive. I may be shy about other things, and I am *not* shy about *this*. The best time to ask for a referral is when the client purchases from you, is happy and excited and wants to tell the world. I simply say, "Who do you know who can benefit from this service?" Then, I describe my ideal client. More often than not, my client comes up with a few people right then. You have grown one client into three or four potential clients with one well-timed question.

Make a point of doing this with every sale!

Create referral rewards. Give your clients a referral reward. Assuming they are satisfied with the service you offer, if they refer three people to you, they get the referral program price. I market a product that is greeting cards and gifts, and have been building my business based on a referral system. My SendOutCards business on the product side has been awesome for building relationships. I send a greeting card with a Starbucks™ gift card to aid in my referral rewards. It has created an awesome referral network.

Where can you create referral rewards?

Hold a contest. If you have a group of raving fans, why not hold a contest? I love this! This is your business, so have fun!

I have a contest about once a quarter and offer a prize to whoever gives me the most referrals. Find out what motivates people to give referrals. Is it coaching time with you, the opportunity to win an iPad® or a gift card? A contest creates buzz with your customers, and they have fun in the process.

Work for the referral. Instead of just giving free appointments or samples of your product or service, give free appointments in return for a few referrals. I have done this in my corporate job, as well as my business. I think it is a great way to enhance your referrals and your value to your clients. For example, if you are a hair stylist, you can provide a hair makeover session that helps the client see what style works best for them and, at the same time, you get a few referrals from her.

Give referral gift cards. Add referral gift cards or certificates for your product or service to your email newsletter. This will keep your product or service at top of mind of your clients and network.

Note: If you are not doing an email newsletter to give your clients updates, I would advise you to start one. Do not bombard your clients with emails. Just keep them up to date and provide value with your products or services.

Show appreciation. Have customer appreciation days. Everyone wants to be appreciated. In my business, I am the appreciation queen! It has been easier to grow my business from my current clients than to use paid advertising. Host a party in honor of your customers and clients, send small gifts and cards, clip and mail articles you think will interest them.

Get Moving!

I have rubbed shoulders with the best businesspeople of the world. One thing I learned from each of them is to develop the relationships in your network. Your network and connections can provide you with a recession-proof business. Build the relationships, create friendships and network for life—and for your business.

Special *Woman Entrepreneur Extraordinaire* Offer

Go to www.thesalesjeanie.com for five sales tips to increase your sales in 30 days.

JEANIE BREISINGER

(480) 382-1317
info@thesalesjeanie.com
www.thesalesjeanie.com

Jeanie Breisinger had been a top producer in the pharmaceutical industry for more than ten years before deciding to become an entrepreneur. She chose a network marketing company and quickly found a few mentors, shot up through the ranks and won many prestigious incentive trips, along with the ability to create the elusive residual income we are all looking for. There were some similarities why Jeanie did well both in pharmaceutical sales and network marketing. She was good at sales, good at understanding people, and good at being coachable.

Jeanie coaches her clients on relationship marketing using online and offline techniques with the goal to develop better relationships. She is a managing director of eWomen Network™ in Tucson, Arizona. This has helped her connect women business owners with each other to grow their businesses and give back to their communities. Jeanie is a speaker, coach and a co-author.

Passionate about showing business professionals how to develop powerful relationships using offline and online strategies, Jeanie provides her clients and students with a proven turnkey business model that is perfect for entrepreneurs, corporations and small business owners.

More
WOMAN ENTREPRENEUR
Extraordinaire!

Now that you have learned many things about how to become a woman entrepreneur extraordinaire with a wide variety of tips, techniques and strategies, the next step is to take action. Get started applying what you have learned in the pages of this book.

We want you to know that we are here to help you meet your professional and personal objectives. Below is a list of where we are geographically located. Regardless of where our companies are located, many of us provide a variety of services over the phone or through webinars, and we welcome the opportunity to travel to your location.

You can find out more about each of us by reading our bios at the end of our chapters, or by visiting our websites listed on the next pages. When you are ready for one-on-one consulting or group training from any of the co-authors in this book—we are available! If you call us and let us know you have read our book, we will provide you with a free phone consultation to determine your needs and how we can best serve you.

United States

Arizona
Jeanie Breisinger   www.thesalesjeanie.com

California
Sheri Brunnquell   www.thesilvergal.com
Yvette Ervin   www.beautyfullofcolor.com
V. Lynn Hawkins   www.skyhawkenterprisesonline.com
Dortha Hise   www.dorthahise.com
LynAnn King   www.kingsingspr.com
Arlene Krantz   www.arlenekrantz.com
Beverly Lenz   www.beliefchangesystems.com
Nancy Lewellen   www.palladianlawgroup.com
LaNette Parker   www.lanetteparker.com
Caterina Rando   www.caterinarando.com
Tammy Tribble   www.mimeticdesigns.com

Connecticut
Sylvia Guinan   www.sylviaguinan.wfadv.com

Florida
Heather Calma   www.heathercalma.com

Louisiana
Michele Scism   www.decisiveminds.com

Massachusetts
Lisa Centamore Sinkiewicz   www.lisasinkiewicz.com

New York
Georgina Sweeney   www.georginasweeney.com

Pennsylvania

Melanie Fitzpatrick   www.empoweringimages.com

Texas

Alice Hinckley   www.yourlightbulbmoments.com
Elizabeth McCormick www.yourinspirationalspeaker.com

Canada

Quebec

Simone Hoa   www.passion2success.com

Become a Published Author with THRIVE Publishing

THRIVE Publishing develops books for experts who want to share their knowledge with more and more people. We can help you become a published author to showcase your expertise, build your list and advance your business and career.

We realize that getting a book written and published is a huge undertaking, and we make that process as easy as possible. We have an experienced team of professionals with the resources and knowledge to put a quality, informative book in your hands quickly and affordably.

We also partner with organizations or institutions to publish books that would be of interest to their members. In this case, sales of the book can be a revenue stream/fundraiser for the organization. A book can enhance your mission, give you a professional outreach tool and enable you to communicate essential information to a wider audience.

Contact us to discuss how we can work together
on your book project.

Phone: 415-668-4535
email: info@thrivebooks.com

Is it time for yours?

415-668-4535
www.thrivebooks.com

Also from
THRIVE Publishing™

For more information
on this book, visit
www.executiveimagebook.com

For more information
on this book, visit
www.execetiquette.com

For more information
on this book, visit
www.directsellingbook.com

For more information
on this book, visit
www.getorganizedtodaybook.com

Also from
THRIVE Publishing™

For more information
on this book, visit
www.incrediblebusinessbook.com

For more information
on this book, visit
www.mystylemywaybook.com

For more information
on this book, visit
www.momentrepreneurbook.com

For more information
on this book, visit
www.powerofcivilitybook.com

Also from
THRIVE Publishing™

For more information
on this book, visit
www.makeyourconnectionscount.com

For more information
on this book, visit
www.savvyleadership.com

For more information
on this book, visit
www.latinnovating.com

For more information
on this book, visit
www.directsellers.com

For more copies of this book, *Woman Entrepreneur Extraordinaire*,
contact any of the co-authors or visit
www.womanentrepreneurbook.com